Japanese Religion

James M. Vardaman

Level 5

IBC パブリッシング

本書は、2011年に弊社から刊行された対訳ニッポン双書『外国人によく聞かれる 日本の宗教』の英文から項目をセレクトし、一部改訂したものです。

はじめに

　ラダーシリーズは、「はしご (ladder)」を使って一歩一歩上を目指すように、学習者の実力に合わせ、無理なくステップアップできるよう開発された英文リーダーのシリーズです。

　リーディング力をつけるためには、繰り返したくさん読むこと、いわゆる「多読」がもっとも効果的な学習法であると言われています。多読では、「1. 速く 2. 訳さず英語のまま 3. なるべく辞書を使わず」に読むことが大切です。スピードを計るなど、速く読むよう心がけましょう（たとえば TOEIC® テストの音声スピードはおよそ 1 分間に 150語です）。そして 1 語ずつ訳すのではなく、英語を英語のまま理解するくせをつけるようにします。こうして読み続けるうちに語感がついてきて、だんだんと英語が理解できるようになるのです。まずは、ラダーシリーズの中からあなたのレベルに合った本を選び、少しずつ英文に慣れ親しんでください。たくさんの本を手にとるうちに、英文書がすらすら読めるようになってくるはずです。

《**本シリーズの特徴**》

- 中学校レベルから中級者レベルまで5段階に分かれています。自分に合ったレベルからスタートしてください。

- クラシックから現代文学、ノンフィクション、ビジネスと幅広いジャンルを扱っています。あなたの興味に合わせてタイトルを選べます。

- 巻末のワードリストで、いつでもどこでも単語の意味を確認できます。レベル1、2では、文中の全ての単語が、レベル3以上は中学校レベル外の単語が掲載されています。

- カバーにヘッドホーンマークのついているタイトルは、オーディオ・サポートがあります。ウェブから購入／ダウンロードし、リスニング教材としても併用できます。

《**使用語彙について**》

レベル1：中学校で学習する単語約1000語

レベル2：レベル1の単語＋使用頻度の高い単語約300語

レベル3：レベル1の単語＋使用頻度の高い単語約600語

レベル4：レベル1の単語＋使用頻度の高い単語約1000語

レベル5：語彙制限なし

CONTENTS

Introduction to Japanese Religion

The following questions and answers are a bit more difficult than those in the main part of this book. Therefore, the language is somewhat more challenging. But these are questions that most foreign visitors to Japan will wonder about, so we will consider them here at the very start.

◼ Are the Japanese religious?

Japanese tend to say that they are not religious. This is partly because the majority does not make a conscious decision to "join" a religious group. And it is partly because most do not pay much attention to the doctrines of the sects of Buddhism or the details of the *kami* of the Shinto shrines they visit.

However, they do participate in "religious" events such as *hatsumode* (the first visit of the year to a shrine or temple) and *ohaka mairi* (visiting the family tomb). They do pray for good health, success on examinations and prosperity in business.

It is safe to say that they are not religious in the Western sense. But they are religious in a cultural sense that is somewhat unique to Japan.

◼ Are the Japanese Buddhists?

During the Tokugawa period (1603–1868), every member of every family became "Buddhist." They were required to do this by the Bakufu, the military government. The Bakufu felt Christianity was a dangerous religion and suppressed it. The Bakufu required Japanese to prove that they were *not* Christian, by having them register as a parishioner of a Buddhist temple.

Without a formal registration, people could not register marriages or get official passes for travel outside the local area. They would also be suspected of believing in Christianity. So, each family naturally went to the closest temple, a popular temple not too far away, or a temple with a popular priest and registered every member of the family as a parishioner. The temples received support only from their members. It came in the form of donations, made on occasions such as funerals and memorial services. This created the idea that Buddhism is primarily a religion related to death.

This system also turned the Buddhist priests into civil servants. Their job was not to preach Buddhism, lead people to enlightenment, or help them in times of trouble. Their job was to register local residents and keep track of them for the government. As a result, Buddhism lost its vitality and many people came to resent the priests and temples. However, the local temple priest did perform a valuable service for members: holding funeral rites.

Japanese today may not know which sect their "family temple" belongs to. It does not really matter to them. They may not know the particular teachings of that sect or other sects. And they have few occasions or little motivation to learn about Buddhism—until they get closer to the end or their life or until a close family member dies.

■ Why do Japanese go to both shrines and temples?

Basically Japanese are not exclusive when it comes to religion. *Kami*, Buddhas and other spirits have *riyaku*—powers and benefits that can be passed on to human beings. So, most Japanese do not hesitate to pray to Shinto *kami* for health, visit Buddhist temples at New Years and be married in a Christian-style wedding ceremony. They see no conflict in this at all.

However, it is important to realize that participation in such actions is rather casual. Participating in these various "religious" events does not require a commitment to a particular belief or to a particular sect of a religion. You simply ask for help, benefit or protection or express gratitude by means of prayer, ritual, chanting or visiting a place of worship. Throughout history, Japanese have done this. They are simply maintaining that tradition.

CHAPTER 1

Folk Beliefs
and Nature Worship

Chapter 1
民間信仰と自然崇拝

　古代の日本人は、自然のいたるところに神が宿り、森羅万象をつかさどっていると信じていました。人々は自然と自然の持つ力を畏れ、敬いました。川や滝、海では心身を洗い清める「祓い」が行われ、山はとりわけ重要な崇拝対象となりました。

　自然が神聖視されたのは、神が創ったものだからという理由だけではありませんでした。古代日本人は、美しい自然そのものが神聖だと考えていたのです。そのため、自然の力を秘めた美しい場所に神社が建てられました。

　古代人のように熱心な信仰ではないものの、自然崇拝は今も日本人の信仰心の根底に息づいています。

キーワード

- ☐ Benzaiten 弁財天
- ☐ Bishamonten 毘沙門天
- ☐ Daikokuten 大黒天
- ☐ Ebisu 恵比寿
- ☐ Fukurokuju 福禄寿
- ☐ goryo 御霊
- ☐ Hotei 布袋
- ☐ itako イタコ
- ☐ Jurojin 寿老人
- ☐ onryo 怨霊
- ☐ Shichifukujin 七福神
- ☐ Sugawara no Michizane 菅原道真
- ☐ ta-no-kami 田の神
- ☐ Taira no Masakado 平将門
- ☐ tengu 天狗
- ☐ yama-no-kami 山の神

◼ What are the characteristics of Japanese nature worship?

Ancient Japanese believed nature was the place where *kami* lived and interacted between heaven and earth. They had a deep appreciation and respect for nature and its powers. They used rivers, waterfalls and the ocean to perform purification (*harai*). Mountain worship became especially important.

These ancient people believed nature was sacred not just because it was created by the *kami*. They believed that places of beauty were sacred by themselves. Therefore, they created shrines at sites of natural power and beauty.

Today nature worship underlies Japanese religiosity, even though it is not as obvious as it was in ancient times.

◼ What are the *yama-no-kami* and *ta-no-kami*?

In ancient Japan, people believed that deities (*kami*) lived on the tops of mountains. During the rice-growing season, the *yama-no-kami* (mountain deities) came down to the fields from the spring planting to the autumn harvest. Farmers greeted them as the local *ta-no-kami*, deities of the fields, with a festival in the spring. At harvest time, the farmers expressed their gratitude to the deities, which then returned to the mountains.

◾ What is mountain worship?

Mountains were long worshipped for three reasons. First, they were considered to be *kami* (deities). Second, they were considered to be places where deities live. These deities included the spirits of the dead who assisted the living. They also included *ta-no-kami*, the *kami* of the rice fields, who descended to the fields in the spring and return to the mountains after the harvest. Third, they were closer to the "other world." It is easier to communicate with the spirits of the dead from the top of a mountain.

Mountains such as Mt. Ontake (on the border of Nagano and Gifu prefectures), Mt. Osore (Aomori prefecture) and Mt. Fuji were considered especially auspicious. In ancient times, people worshipped Mt. Fuji as a female mountain deity. In the Heian period, Mt. Fuji became a center of *Shugendo*, a kind of mountain worship. Climbing Mt. Fuji has been a religious act for centuries, and it is often seen as an act of purification.

◼ What is a "vengeful spirit"?

"Vengeful spirits," *onryo* or *goryo*, are the evil spirits of people of high rank who were either killed or died in anger. The curse of vengeful spirits was held to take the form of natural calamities, such as earthquakes, lightning and typhoons. Among the most famous of these supposed spirits are two from the Heian period.

Sugawara no Michizane (845–903) opposed the power of the Fujiwara family. He was falsely accused of plotting against the imperial court. As a result, he was sent into exile at Dazaifu in Kyushu. He died there after writing a series of famous poems protesting his innocence. After his death, a number of misfortunes occurred at the court in Kyoto, including fire, flood, and unexpected deaths. Some people believed these misfortunes were caused by his angry spirit, which was trying to get vengeance against those who had wronged him.

They tried to soothe his angry spirit in several ways. He was posthumously pardoned and even promoted to the highest of court ranks in an effort to calm his anger. Kitano Shrine in Kyoto and Dazaifu Shrine in Dazaifu were dedicated to him, and he was deified as Tenman Tenjin. Over the centuries he has evolved into the benign patron of calligraphy and culture.

Taira no Masakado (unknown–940) led a major rebellion of warriors from the Kanto area against the central government. In 940 what had begun as a local conflict turned into rebellion against the government, when Masakado attacked and occupied government quarters and installed his own administrators. He attempted to make the Kanto area into an independent state, with himself as emperor. His rebellion was crushed and he was killed. He later came to be worshipped at Kanda Myojin in present-day Tokyo.

■ What is special about Osorezan?

Mt. Osore (Osorezan) is in northeastern Aomori prefecture. The mountain is sacred to both shamans and Buddhists. On the banks of the caldera lake is Entsuji temple, said to date from the 9th century. There is a bridge representing the entrance to the afterworld.

There are also small stones piled by parents who have come to pray for the spirits of their children who died young. There are

Mt. Osore (Aomori)

also small statues of Jizo, with caps and bibs, and pinwheels.

Mediums known as *itako* gather here July 20–24. Upon request, these women communicate with the deceased. Both the *itako* and their clients are decreasing in number.

■ What is a *tengu*?

A *tengu* is a half-bird, half-man creature from Japanese folklore. He has a man's body, arms and legs, a red face, and wings. He also has a long nose and brushy eyebrows. *Tengu* masks are often painted red and have eyes that glitter. They are sometimes sold at inns and shops in the countryside as talismans.

Basically the *tengu* is the bodily form of a *yama-no-kami*, the guardian of a particular mountain. He is feared for his supernatural powers, but may also be seen as a protector. The *tengu* is associated with the *yamabushi*, ascetics who also live and practice rites in the mountains. Often *tengu* are shown wearing items of the distinctive costume of the *yamabushi*.

◾ Who are the Seven Deities of Good Fortune?

The Seven Deities of Good Fortune, *Shichifukujin*, became popular during the 15th through 17th centuries. They include Hindu, Buddhist and Daoist deities and sages from India, China and Japan. They are usually pictured riding on a treasure ship, *takarabune*.

Bishamonten (India) is the god of warriors and protects against harm and injury.

Daikokuten (India) protects farmers and the kitchen and prevents floods. This deity is often shown with a magic mallet and mice, which increase during a good harvest.

① Ebisu
② Jurojin
③ Daikokuten
④ Fukurokuju
⑤ Bishamonten
⑥ Hotei
⑦ Benzaiten

Benzaiten (India), the only female deity, is the patron of music, literature and the arts.

Fukurokuju (China) is the deity of long life and fertility. He is often shown with a drinking gourd and a scroll which is inscribed the wisdom of the world.

Hotei (China) is the deity of happiness and contentment. He is also called the Laughing Buddha, and rubbing his stomach is said to bring good luck.

Jurojin (China) brings long life and good fortune. He carries a drinking gourd filled with rice wine.

Ebisu (Japan) is the deity who protects fishermen, business and wealth. He is often shown with a sea bream (*tai*) which symbolizes congratulations.

CHAPTER 2

Shinto

Kazahino-minomiyabashi of Ise Jingu (Mie)

Chapter 2
神道

　神道は一般に宗教ととらえられていますが、仏教やキリスト教などのいわゆる世界宗教とは性格が異なります。神道には創始者がいませんし、経典や体系だった教義もありません。

　もともと神道は、自然現象や祖先、多様な神々を崇拝する古代の信仰が融合して生まれたもので、信仰に呼び名はありませんでした。しかし中国から仏教が伝来すると、仏教との区別をはかるため、「神の道」を意味する神道という名称で呼ばれるようになりました。

　神道は日常の暮らし、とくに農村の暮らしの中に取り込まれていきました。現在の日本人の暮らしにもその名残があるのは、神道が前向きな考え方や清らかさ、祈願を重んじる、親しみやすい信仰だからでしょう。

キーワード

- ☐ Amaterasu 天照大御神
- ☐ Hachiman 八幡
- ☐ Inari 稲荷
- ☐ Izanagi no Mikoto イザナギノミコト
- ☐ Izanami no Mikoto イザナミノミコト
- ☐ Kokka Shinto 国家神道
- ☐ miko 巫女
- ☐ Minamoto no Yoritomo 源頼朝
- ☐ sumo 相撲
- ☐ Susanoo no Mikoto スサノオノミコト
- ☐ tatari 祟り
- ☐ Tokugawa Ieyasu 徳川家康
- ☐ yakudoshi 厄年
- ☐ yao-yorozu-no-kami 八百万の神
- ☐ Yasukuni Shrine 靖国神社
- ☐ Yomi no Kuni 黄泉の国

◪ How did Shinto develop?

While Shinto is usually treated as a religion, it is different from most so-called world religions. It does not have a founder. It does not have real scriptures. And it does not have a system of doctrines.

Basically it evolved out of the ancient worship of unique natural phenomena, ancestors and various kinds of *kami*. This worship did not need to have a name until it was confronted by Buddhism, which was imported from China. Eventually it came to be called Shinto, "the way of the deities," to distinguish it from the newly introduced Buddhism.

Shinto existed side by side with Buddhism. Sometimes its *kami* were said to be manifestations of buddhas. Sometimes the two religions became involved in political conflicts. But as a general rule, Shinto continued to be an integral part of everyday life, especially in farming communities. It remains part of Japanese life, partly because it focuses on positive beliefs, purity and hopeful wishes. This makes it accessible to anyone, at any level of belief.

◲ What is a *kami*?

Defining *kami* is not easy. It is best to think of a *kami* as something that produces the emotions of awe or fear. A *kami* can be positive or negative, but it always possesses a miraculous, mysterious power. A *kami* is either the power itself or something that possesses such power. Rather than translating *kami* as "god/gods," it is safer to translate it as "deity/deities."

Japanese tradition refers to *yao-yorozu-no-kami*, which means "myriads of deities." But there are two main categories of *kami*. One kind is the heavenly or earthly *kami* mentioned in Japanese mythology. The other includes those connected with natural phenomena, those connected with historical people and those who are connected with prosperity, commerce and occupations. Farmers, fishermen, and hunters each have their own deities.

The Tomb of Tokugawa Ieyasu in Nikko Toshogu (Tochigi)

Natural phenomena that are considered *kami* are Mt. Fuji, other impressive mountains, waterfalls, peculiar rocks, unique or ancient trees, thunder and lightning. In the animal world, deer, snakes and foxes are considered *kami*. Among humans, over a period of time, the 9th-century court scholar Sugawara no Michizane became deified as Tenman Tenjin, patron saint of scholarship. The first Tokugawa shogun, Tokugawa Ieyasu, was deified as Daigongen at the Toshogu shrine at Nikko.

▣ What *kami* are mentioned in mythology?

The *Kojiki* (Record of Ancient Matters, 712) is the oldest existing chronicle of Japan. It records the mythology of the creation of heaven and earth and the founding of Japan. It tells how the male deity Izanagi no Mikoto and the female deity Izanami no Mikoto stood on the Floating Bridge of Heaven and stuck the Heavenly Jeweled Spear into the ocean below the bridge. The water from that spear formed an island. On the island the two carried out the rites of marriage.

Izanami gave birth to the islands of Japan and their various deities. When she gave birth to the fire deity, she was burned and died. Deeply saddened, Izanagi followed her into the underworld, *Yomi no Kuni*, and found her in a terrible state. She pleads with him not to look at her. But he does, and out of shame and anger, she pursues him back to the entrance to the underworld. He barely escapes, then pushes a boulder across the entrance, separating the world of the living from the world of the dead. He carries out a purification rite which produces the Sun Goddess, Amaterasu, and her brother Susanoo no Mikoto. Amaterasu became the principal female deity of Shinto mythology.

◼ What kind of *kami* is Hachiman?

Hachiman is revered as the *kami* of warriors and the community. An oracle announced that Hachiman would protect the construction of the Great Buddha (*daibutsu*) at Nara, completed in 752. From that time on, Hachiman was seen as a Shinto protector of Buddhism. The *kami* was given the Buddhist name *Daibosatsu*, meaning "Great Bodhisattva."

Hachiman became the tutelary *kami* of the Minamoto, a powerful military clan. When Minamoto no Yoritomo (1147–1199) established the shogunate at Kamakura, he wanted to strengthen his claim to power. He did this by building a shrine to Hachiman in the city. Named Tsurugaoka Hachimangu, it is the main Hachiman Shrine in eastern Japan. There are reported

Tsurugaoka Hachimangu
(Kanagawa)

to be close to 30,000 smaller shrines to Hachiman around the country.

◼ What kind of *kami* is *Inari*?

Inari is one of the names of the deity of cereals or grains, which of course includes rice. Because *Inari* is associated with agriculture, it is also a guardian of commerce. During the Edo period (1603–1868), *Inari* shrines were built by those hoping for prosperity and success. Today *Inari* is taken as the deity of even large companies, and head offices may have an *Inari* shrine on the property. There may be as many as 30,000 *Inari* shrines throughout Japan.

In medieval Japan, it was believed that white foxes were sacred messengers of *Inari*. The fox also came to be called *inari*. Because it was believed that the fox's favorite food was fried soybean curd, it also came to be called *inari*.

Fox Statue at Fushimi Inari Taisha (Kyoto)

◼ What are the characteristics of a shrine?

Shinto shrines are enclosed sacred areas. The entrance usually has a *torii* gate. Inside the gate may be two stone *komainu* (Korean dog) sculptures that protect the shrine. The building facing the gate is a worship hall, *haiden*, and behind it is the main sanctuary, *honden*.

In front of the worship hall is a wooden box to receive money offerings from visitors. This is where worshippers announce that they have come to worship. They do this by pulling on a heavy rope to make a sound with the bell (*suzu*) and by making a good sound by clapping their hands, usually twice.

Shrine Compound

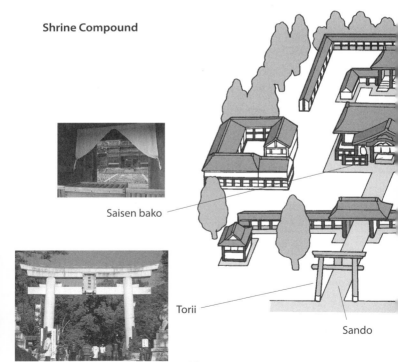

Saisen bako

Torii

Sando

The *haiden* is where priests carry out ceremonies and rituals. The *honden* contains the sacred object in which the spirit of the deity is believed to reside.

There may also be a stage or hall (*kaguraden*) for sacred dance and music (*kagura*).

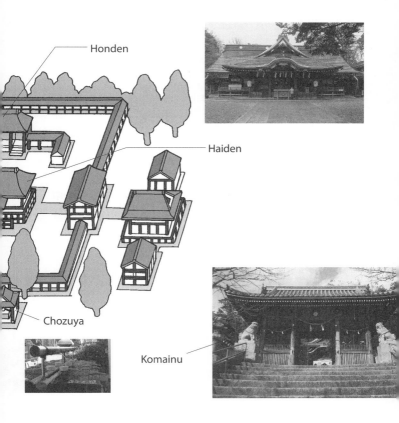

Honden

Haiden

Chozuya

Komainu

Meiji Jingu (Tokyo)

Izumo Taisha (Shimane)

◼ What is the difference between *jinja*, *jingu* and *taisha*?

Jinja (shrine) is the overall name for places where a *kami* (divine spirit) resides and where rituals are performed. *Jingu* is the name for certain shrines that have some connection with the imperial house. The most famous examples are Meiji Jingu in Tokyo and Ise Jingu in Mie prefecture. *Taisha* is the term for a shrine used for Izumo Taisha, a particularly important shrine in Shimane prefecture.

◼ What is a matsuri?

Essentially matsuri (festivals) are ceremonial occasions of Shinto origin. They are chiefly related to rice cultivation and the spiritual well-being of the local community. They have their origin in Shinto rites to please the gods and the spirits of the dead.

The basic rites are prayers for a successful

harvest, prayers of thanksgiving and prayers for the prevention of disasters or pestilence. These rites are symbolic acts of communication between the local people and the local *kami*. This involves the whole community and usually involves some form of shared feast.

The term matsuri is also borrowed and used to describe special events that are newly created and have no Shinto background.

▣ What is a *mikoshi*?

Mikoshi are "portable shrines" that carry the *kami* from a shrine through the streets of the community during a festival. They are usually carried on the shoulders of the participants. They range from small palanquins that children can carry or pull to huge palanquins weighing over a ton.

During some festivals, the *mikoshi* may be carried into the sea or loaded onto a boat and carried to various locations before returning to the shrine.

▣ What is a *torii*?

A *torii* is a gate to the entrance of a shrine compound. It has a crossbeam at the top, which is sometimes curved and sometimes flat. It is not necessary to walk through the gate.

There are some 20 different styles of *torii*, each matching the style of the shrine buildings. If you look at these closely you can tell which *kami* is enshrined in it.

The Great Torii Gate of Heian Jingu (kyoto)

■ What is a *shimenawa*?

A *shimenawa* is a rope made of twisted strands of rice straw. When decorated with white paper, it marks a sacred space. It is believed to have the power to ward off evil and sickness.

A *shimenawa* may be placed around a distinctive tree or rock, especially within the area surrounding a shrine. One may be placed at the entrance to a Shinto shrine. The most well-known is an enormous *shimenawa* that hangs before the kaguraden of Izumo Taisha in Shimane prefecture. It is 13 meters long and 9 meters in circumference. It weighs 5 tons.

Shimenawa at the Kaguraden of Izumo Taisha (Shimane)

In professional sumo a Grand Champion wears a specially tied white *shimenawa* as an essential part of his outfit in certain ceremonies.

◼ What are *kamishide* used for?

Kamishide are zigzag strips of paper. They indicate the presence of a deity at a shrine. They may hang from a piece of rope or a vertical post. They are also attached to a wooden stick or to a branch of sakaki that is offered to the *kami* in formal rites. Most *kamishide* are made of simple white paper, while others are made of special gold paper, cotton cloth or gilt metal.

◼ What are the bells used for?

Above the wooden box for offerings at many shrines is a thick rope connected to a bell. People shake the rope to make noise with the bell in order to call the deity. Making a sound by clapping the hands together, called *kashiwade*, is another part of making your presence known to the deity.

◼ What is *kagura*?

Kagura, sacred music and masked dance, is performed at major shrines to pacify and entertain the deity. It is also performed as part of local festivals and at rituals at the imperial court. It dates from at least the 9th century. It is now considered part of Japanese folk performing arts (*minzoku geino*).

■ How do you worship at a shrine?

First, at the *chozuya* you rinse your hands and mouth. Go to the main hall (*haiden*) and drop a coin in the offering box (*saisen-bako*). The next step

① Make two deep bows.

is slightly different at each shrine. At Ise Shrine, for example, you make two deep bows, clap your hands twice, then make one final deep bow. Other shrines call for three or four claps. This clapping, called *kashiwade*, is believed to be the proper way to get the attention of the deity of the shrine.

On your way out after worshipping, you may buy a talisman or an *ema* plaque at the shrine office.

③ Make a final deep bow.

② Make two loud claps of the hands at chest height.

◼ What is the purpose of *osaisen*?

In front of the main hall of shrines and temples is a wooden box with a grill on top, called a *saisen-bako*. Visitors throw coins or bills into it as an offering, when they pray for something, especially at the beginning of the New Year.

There is no set amount for an offering, but people often use a kind of word play to set the amount. A large donation of ¥2,951 (which could be read as *fu-ku-ko-i*) could be offered with the wish "Good luck, come!" (*fuku koi*). A much more common donation would be a single ¥5 (*go-en*) coin. The word play here is that *goen* could also mean "having a bond with the deity or buddha."

◼ What is a *miko*?

There are two kinds of *miko*. In ancient times, a *miko* was a woman who possessed special magical powers. She could call forth the divine power of the *kami* and announce oracles from the *kami*. She could also help the living communicate with their dead ancestors. The mediums called *itako*, who

Chihaya

Hibakama

gather at Mt. Osore, come from this tradition.

The contemporary *miko* is a woman who assists the priest of a shrine in ritual and clerical duties. During Shinto festivals and ceremonies, you may see four *miko* performing a dance. They usually wear a white kimono and loose red trousers called *hakama*. They may also wear a special form of cassock (*chihaya*) with chrysanthemums as a headdress.

▣ What is *hatsu miya mairi*?

A child's first visit to a shrine is called *hatsu miya mairi*. It is the first time that a family presents the child to the *kami* of a shrine. The first visit by baby boys is the 32nd day after birth. The first visit by baby girls is the 33rd day. In the past, childbirth was considered to leave the mother in a condition of "impurity." Therefore, the child's father and grand-mother presented the child to the *kami*. Nowadays, the mother usually participates.

Rites during this visit include prayers chanted by a priest, a dance performed by a *miko* and a blessing of the child.

▣ What is *tatari*?

Tatari means "misfortune." It comes as a punishment or as a warning from a *kami* that is angered by something a human has done or said. It requires purification by a ritual like that described in the section above.

◾ What is *yakudoshi*? How do you avoid danger from it?

Unlucky years, *yakudoshi*, are ages when a person is most likely to experience misfortune or danger. For women, the ages 19, 33 (especially), 61, and 70, and for men, the ages 25, 42 (especially), 61, and 70 are considered especially critical. To avoid misfortune during these potentially risky years, some Japanese go to shrines to have a priest perform a purification ceremony to protect them during the dangerous year.

◾ What are *norito*?

Norito are a kind of Shinto prayer. They are sacred forms of speech used when speaking to the deities during shrine rites. They are based on the idea of *koto-dama*, which means the soul or energy of words. Some express gratitude. Some ask for protection or a blessing. Some are prayers for individuals. Nowadays priests do not compose their own but use the *norito* in standard collections from the 19th century.

◼ What is *yomi no kuni* like in Shinto?

In ancient Shinto, *yomi no kuni*, or the afterworld, was considered a place of darkness and the realm of the dead. But the afterworld was connected with the realm of the living. People in the realm of the dead and the realm of the living could communicate with one another. In Shinto there is no idea of punishment after death, so *yomi no kuni* is different from "hell" found in Buddhism or Christianity.

Today, very few Japanese believe in an afterworld.

◼ What kind of offerings do people make at shrines?

Offerings are made to the deities to create a sense of goodwill and beneficence in the deity. Common offerings include food, sweets, fruit and even small bottles of sake.

In a formal ceremony, a common offering is a sprig of sakaki leaves, called *tama-gushi*, which has strips of paper attached to it. In a ritual led by a priest, each participant puts one sprig on a small table set up before the symbol of the deity.

◼ What is *kegare*?

Kegare refers to different kinds of "impurity," "pollution" or "defilement." *Kegare* is caused by child-bearing, menstruation, disease and death. It is considered to be "a feeling of uncleanliness or impurity." This is not the same as having committed a sin.

These "impurities" affect the individual and people around the individual, including family members. If *kegare* is ignored, then a misfortune (*tatari*) may occur as a warning. In order to eliminate *kegare*, one should perform a purification ritual.

◼ How is "purification" (*oharai* or *misogi*) carried out?

A person can remove impurities (*kegare*) by purification (*oharai*). The purpose of purification is to restore purity, which is the basis of communion with the deities. When the heart, or *kokoro*, is pure, then all of one's actions become proper.

Purification can be done in three different ways. First, a priest can symbolically purify a person or place by waving a wand of paper streamers (*tama-gushi*). Second, one can purify oneself using water (*misogi harai*). In the past, people did this in the sea, in a river or under a waterfall. Saltwater was considered particularly effective. The most common form today is done by washing one's hands with water before entering a shrine. A third way to purify one's self is by abstaining and fasting (*imi*).

A place can be purified by scattering salt on it or sprinkling it with water. Some restaurants and bars place two small piles of salt, called *morishio*, outside the door to their business, one on each side. This custom is less to purify than to welcome customers.

Participants in a Buddhist funeral service may sprinkle salt on themselves before entering their home. This is believed to prevent the "pollution" of death from entering the home of the mourner.

A less common form of purification is by waving the smoke of incense over the body.

▣ What is an *ema*?

Ema are small wooden plaques sold at shrine offices. The word *ema* originally meant "picture of a horse," and the plaques actually had a horse painted on them. This reflects an ancient custom of offering a horse to the deities of certain shrines.

Present-day *ema* have the name of the shrine and some unique design on it. The design may be the current year's animal according to the Chinese zodiac or a design of the shrine. The back is blank so that people can write a petition to the shrine's deity for assistance in achieving some objective. Kitano Tenmangu (Kyoto) and Yushima Tenjin (Tokyo) enshrine the spirit of Sugawara no Michizane, the patron of learning. Students preparing for entrance exams often visit this shrine and buy one of the *ema*. They write their hopes for success in getting into a good school on the back and hang it on the racks that are placed for that purpose.

▣ What is an *omikuji* and what does it tell you?

The drawing of *omikuji*, oracle lots that predict the future, is an ancient custom that came from China. These paper lots are commonly found at both Buddhist temples and Shinto shrines. Lots may be drawn by shaking a stick out of a container and using the mark on the stick to select a fortune written on paper. Or a lot may be drawn directly from a box. Either way, this random selection is understood to be the guidance of the buddhas or deities. Japanese often draw lots at the beginning of the year.

Actual *omikuji*, literally "sacred lots," are long rolled-up strips of paper. Each has one of a dozen or so overall oracles, such as *daikichi* (great blessing or great fortune), *kichi* (blessing or fortune), *kyo* (curse or bad fortune) and *daikyo* (great curse or worst fortune). Each also foretells specific aspects of life, including hopes, romance, travel, illness and business.

Some people tie their paper lot on a tree branch or on wires provided by the temple or shrine. They may hope this will make a good fortune come true or prevent bad luck from occurring. Those who draw a good luck lot may take theirs home as a charm.

◼ What are *ofuda*?

Ofuda are flat pieces of wood, slightly broader and pointed at the top. On them are written the name of the shrine (or temple) and the deity (or buddha) that is worshipped there. *Ofuda* are considered *kamisama no bunshin*, an incarnation of the deity. Each *fuda* is wrapped in a white paper and tied with string. It is placed in the home in order to protect the house and its surroundings.

◼ What are *hamaya*?

Hamaya are "evil-destroying arrows." In the past they were believed to protect against evil spirits. Nowadays they are considered a charm that brings good health and well-being to members of the family. These arrows are available in early January when people make their first visit of the year to shrines.

◪ What are *omamori*?

Omamori are amulets. They are believed to prevent misfortune and to protect a person against danger. An *omamori* is usually a small cloth pouch with drawstrings. You are not supposed to look inside the pouch. Inside is a piece of paper with an inscription or piece of scripture. On the outside is the name of the shrine or temple, with the benefit on the reverse side. There are usually amulets for good health, household safety (*kanai anzen*), transportation safety (*kotsu anzen*), financial success (*shobai hanjo*), and safe birth (*anzan*). You will often see one of these on a child's school satchel or backpack.

◪ What are *kumade*?

A *kumade*, "bear's paw," is an ornamental rake. It is supposed to "rake in" good luck, wealth and customers, so it is popular among traditional drinking establishments and restaurants. Large rakes are decorated extravagantly with auspicious symbols of bells, deities of prosperity, bales of rice, gold coins, cranes, and tortoises.

Markets selling these *kumade* are held at Otori Shrines on festival days in November. There are two or three festival days, called *Tori-no-ichi*, depending on the year.

▣ What is a *kamidana*?

Sometimes called a "god shelf" in English, the *kamidana* is a Shinto altar in the home. It is used to connect the household with a shrine and to honor the spirits of the ancestors.

Offerings of rice, salt, water and sake may be made daily or twice a month. Some people put amulets or *ofuda* from shrines on the altar. The altar may enshrine a deity that protects a particular occupation and also protects a district.

Small altars can also be found in Japanese-style restaurants, railway stations, company offices and sake breweries. This is especially true among more traditional trades and occupations.

▣ What is a *kadomatsu*?

Kadomatsu is a pair of decorations made of three pieces of bamboo and pine branches tied together with straw. They are placed in front of houses and office buildings at the end of the year.

The *kadomatsu* is a seasonal type of *yorishiro*, literally "approach substitute." Its purpose is to attract the *kami* with a place to reside during the

New Year season. In this case, people want to attract *Toshigami-sama*, the deity of the new year. Usually on January 7 the decoration is taken down and placed in a ritual bonfire at a shrine. One well-known ceremony in which New Year's decorations of various kinds are thrown onto a bonfire is the *Donto-sai* at the Osaki Hachiman Shrine in Sendai (Miyagi prefecture).

◼ What is *kagami-mochi*?

Kagami-mochi are large, round cakes of rice. They are made from steamed glutinous rice which is pounded in a wooden mortar with a large wooden mallet. These big flat cakes are made as an offering to *Toshigami-sama*, the god of the new year. They are set on altars with other auspicious New Year decorations.

◼ What is *hatsumode*?

Hatsumode, "the first shrine or temple visit," refers to a person's first visit of the New Year. It is common for Japanese to visit well-known shrines or temples beginning at midnight on New Year's Eve. Often, however, people make this visit sometime during the first three days of the year.

Especially popular are Meiji Shrine (Tokyo),

Tsurugaoka Hachiman Shrine (Kamakura), Kawasaki Daishi (Kanagawa) and Yasaka Shrine (Kyoto).

■ Is *sumo* part of Shinto?

Sumo has been traced to ancient harvest divination. Certain elements in contemporary professional *sumo* are related to Shinto, such as the roof over the ring and its tassels, the throwing of salt, and certain other rituals.

The roof was once supported by four pillars, but they are now represented by tassels. The green tassel represents spring and the green dragon god of the east (*seiryo*). The red tassel represents summer and the red sparrow god of the south (*shujaku*). The white tassel represents autumn and the white tiger god of the west (*byakko*). The black tassel represents winter and the turtle god of the north (*genbu*).

The ring, or *dohyo*, is purified in a Shinto ceremony at the beginning of each tournament. Prior to a bout (*torikumi*) and before entering the ring, each wrestler (*rikishi*) purifies himself by rinsing his mouth with water. He then purifies the ring by throwing salt into it.

All newly promoted Grand Champions, *yokozuna*, perform a formal ritual at Meiji Shrine, which honors the spirit of Emperor Meiji. The *yokozuna* and other top-ranked wrestlers also pay respects at Ise Shrine each spring.

▣ What was "State Shinto," *Kokka Shinto*?

"State Shinto" was not a true religion. It was an attempt to centralize government administration, using religious elements. Beginning with the Meiji Restoration, the new government made use of Shinto ideas, organizations and ceremonies. It encouraged two beliefs: the divinity of the emperor and the uniqueness of Japan's "national essence," or *kokutai*. It turned shrines into places for national ceremonies. In other words, shrines became government institutions. The main purpose of the shrines was to foster patriotism and loyalty. Priests were appointed by the government and citizens were required to register with local shrines.

After World War II, this system was abolished. Today shrines are private religious organizations. But shrines like Yasukuni Shrine still appear to have a semi-government character.

▣ Why is there controversy about Yasukuni Shrine?

Yasukuni Shrine (Tokyo) enshrines the war dead. The main issue surrounding the shrine began in

1979. In that year it was made known that Class-A war criminals, including Prime Minister Tojo Hideki, had been memorialized the year before. From that year onward, various prime ministers visited the shrine. They usually did not say whether they did this as private citizens or as public officials. In 1985, Prime Minister Nakasone announced that he visited the shrine as a government official.

Some foreign governments see this as promoting the military and praising Japan's past. The opposition says that this is just honoring the dead. The issue continues and will not be easily settled.

CHAPTER 3

Connections between Shinto and Buddhism

Three-story Pagoda of Seiganto-ji and Nachi Falls
(Wakayama)

Chapter 3
神道と仏教のつながり

　7世紀に仏教が日本で広まってまもなく、日本人は仏と神を結びつける方法を模索しはじめました。まず、土地を守護する氏神が仏教の守護神として考えられるようになりました。10世紀には、神は仏や菩薩が姿を変えて現れたものであるとされ、13世紀になると主要な神社の祭神の多くが、特定の仏の化身として同一視されるようになりました。

　こうした神仏の同一視から生まれた思想が、本地垂迹で、仏が日本の神々の姿をとって地上に降りてくることを意味しています。仏教を守護する菩薩としても崇められる八幡はその代表例です。寺院の境内に神社が建てられたのは、神道と仏教を一つにまとめるためでした。このことは、単一の宗教にこだわらず、複数の宗教を受け入れる日本人の信仰のあり方をよく表しています。

キーワード

☐ adherent 信者
☐ danka 檀家
☐ haibutsu kishaku 廃仏毀釈
☐ honji suijaku 本地垂迹
☐ incarnation 権化
☐ registrar 戸籍係
☐ shinbutsu bunri 神仏分離

◨ Why are a shrine and a temple sometimes found in the same place?

When Buddhism was introduced to Japan in the 7th century, Japanese almost immediately began to try to find a way to relate buddhas and deities. The local *kami* were seen as protectors of Buddhism. By the 10th century, Shinto deities were taken to be incarnations of buddhas and bodhisattvas. By the 13th century, deities of many major shrines were identified with particular Buddhist deities.

Out of this developed the concept called *honji suijaku*, "original essence, descended manifestation." This means that Shinto deities are Japanese manifestations of buddhas. The best example is the Shinto deity Hachiman, who was taken to be a bodhisattva protecting Buddhism. Shrines were built at temples bringing the two religions together. This "cooperation" is an example of how Japanese tend to accept multiple forms of religion, rather than choosing just one.

◼ Why were Shinto and Buddhism completely separated?

During the Tokugawa period, the government turned Buddhist temples into government agencies. Temples became public registrars. Each person in a specific neighborhood was required to "register" as a member of the local temple. Therefore, the temples served as a kind of government office for controlling the citizens. As a result, Buddhism lost its vitality during this period. Instead, it became primarily associated with funeral ceremonies for members. The new Meiji government in 1868 ordered the separation of Buddhism and Shinto, which is known as *shinbutsu bunri*.

◼ Why was there an anti-Buddhist movement during the Meiji period?

During the Tokugawa period, the government used the Buddhist temples for its own purposes. Many ordinary people resented the power that the temples and priests seemed to have. The new Meiji leaders took this power from the Buddhist temples. These leaders instead began to use Shinto as a way of supporting leadership under the emperor. Using the slogan "eradicate Buddhism," *haibutsu kishaku*, some Shinto followers destroyed priceless

Buddhist temples, sutras and works of art. This anti-Buddhist period ended in 1871, and the two religions remained separate from then on.

◾ Are Japanese today believers in Buddhism or Shintoism?

The Statistical Survey on Religion carried out annually by the Agency of Cultural Affairs reveals amazing statistics. According to the 2019 survey, there are more than 87 million adherents of Shintoism and 84 million adherents of Buddhism in Japan. These numbers do not include the other religions. However, in that year the Japanese population was only 126 million. How is this possible?

Actually, the people counted as "adherents" may not even be aware that they "belong" to a shrine or temple. The number of registered members is provided by the shrines and temples, not by individuals. All members of a temple *danka* are counted, even though the only connection individuals might have with the temple priest involves a funeral.

The numbers suggest that Japanese simultaneously hold several religions at one time. It is safer to say that most Japanese are not actively involved in religious activities. It is also safe to say that they are open to various religious traditions.

Buddhism

The Konpon Chudo (Main Hall) of Enryakuji (Kyoto)

Chapter 4
仏教

　ゴータマ・シッダールタは釈迦族の王子として、老、病、死といった辛さや悲しみを伴うもの一切に触れることがないよう守られてきましたが、最終的には、人間の生にある忌むべきものすべてを見出してしまいます。

　剃髪し出家したシッダールタは、苦行の後、インド北西部のガヤにあった菩提樹の下で瞑想し、悟りに達します。

　釈迦は「悟れる者」として仏陀と呼ばれるようになり、人々に説法を始めます。自身を苦しみから解き放つには「四聖諦（四つの聖なる真理）」を理解せねばならないと仏陀は説きました。

　仏陀はさらに「八正道（八つの正しい行い）」について説き、こうした仏陀による根本の教えが、仏教として知られるようになりました。

キーワード

- [ ] asura 阿修羅
- [ ] Bosatsu 菩薩
- [ ] daruma だるま
- [ ] Gautama Siddharta ゴータマ・シッダールタ
- [ ] Jizo 地蔵
- [ ] Kannon 観音
- [ ] Kukai 空海
- [ ] mandala 曼荼羅
- [ ] mappo 末法
- [ ] Mikkyo 密教
- [ ] Myoo 明王
- [ ] Nichiren 日蓮
- [ ] Nyorai 如来
- [ ] Saicho 最澄
- [ ] Shakyamuni 釈迦牟尼
- [ ] Zen 禅

▣ What is Buddhism?

Gautama Siddharta is also called Shakyamuni, "sage of the Sakya clan." He was born in the 4th or 5th century B.C. As the son of the king of the Sakya clan, he was raised in luxury. He was protected from everything that was depressing, including aging, illness and death. Eventually, however, he discovered on his own all of these unpleasant and disturbing facts about human life.

He shaved his head and set off in search of enlightenment. After years of ascetic practice and study with Hindu masters, he meditated under a bo tree near Gaya, in northeast India, and attained enlightenment. He realized the fundamental truth is that life is suffering. Our suffering comes from different causes such as growing old, not having something we want, and parting from someone we love.

Shakyamuni came to be called the Buddha, "the Awakened One," and he began preaching to others. He preached that in order to free ourselves from suffering, we should understand the Four Noble Truths: the truth of suffering, the truth of the cause of suffering, the truth of the extinguishing of suffering, and the truth of the method of extinguishing suffering. To gain this "enlightenment" or "awakening," we should extinguish all desires and attachments to this world. We can do this by practicing meditation, undergoing spiritual exercises and following the precepts. He then preached the Eightfold Noble Path, the varieties of actual practice one can follow to fulfill the Four Noble Truths. These fundamental teachings came to be known as Buddhism.

Buddhism teaches that all things are impermanent and therefore "empty." By going beyond momentary attachment to the world and gaining a deep understanding of "emptiness," human beings can achieve true peace of mind. This is the compassionate message of Buddhism.

◼ What are the main types of Buddhism?

Buddhism began in India. Several centuries after Shakyamuni reached enlightenment and began teaching, Buddhism spread to various parts of Asia. As it spread, it was influenced differently in each area.

In Southeast Asia, Buddhism focused on priests who spent all of their time in religious practices. Ordinary believers supported them with food and offerings. This tradition became known as Theravada or Hinayana Buddhism. It is also called "the Lesser Vehicle," because salvation is only possible for the community of priests.

Another tradition of Buddhism traveled over the Himalayas into China, eventually reaching Japan. This tradition became known as Mahayana Buddhism, and is also called "the Greater Vehicle." This tradition believes all living beings have *bussho*, buddha nature, and can become a buddha. It also teaches that gaining salvation for oneself is not enough. One should seek salvation for all living beings.

■ How did Buddhism come to Japan?

Around the 5th century, Indian Buddhist priests began traveling to China, and Chinese priests began traveling to India. Buddhist teachings reached the Korean peninsula from China in 372. The official transmission of Buddhism to Japan is described in the *Nihon Shoki*, the "Chronicle of Japan." It says Emperor Kimmei of Japan received an image of the Buddha and sutras from the Korean peninsula sometime between 538 and 552. Of course, Buddhists from China and Korea had established places of worship in Japan before that, too.

Prince Shotoku, Shotoku Taishi (574–622), is credited with promoting Buddhism, supporting the building of Buddhist temples, and writing commentaries on sutras.

■ How was Buddhism received in Nara and Heian periods?

When Buddhism first arrived in Japan, it was adopted by the imperial court and the nobility. Priests were not allowed to teach the common people.

The first Buddhist priests were basically civil employees. They received salaries from the government. Their occupation was to carry out ceremonies and pray for the safety and peace of the nation. Japanese of that day believed that epidemics were caused by *onryo*, vengeful spirits. So these priests were called on to offer Buddhist prayers to pacify the spirits that caused epidemics. Their prayers were also believed to make crops grow and stop uprisings against the imperial court.

In other words, the government used Buddhism to protect itself, and it strictly controlled Buddhist priests, temples and teachings. Buddhism at this time was not a religion for all the Japanese people. It was only for the elite. In fact, Buddhist priests were not allowed to have contact with the common people. This prevented a priest from becoming a leader of any kind of popular movement that might oppose the government. It was only later that priests began to spread Buddhism among the common people.

■ How did Buddhism change between the Nara and Heian periods?

When Buddhism arrived in Japan, the capital was at Nara. The imperial court sponsored six different teachings which are now referred to as "the Six Nara Schools of Buddhism." They are called schools, because students of Buddhism could focus on several forms of teaching instead of just one. The headquarters for all of them was at Todaiji.

Buddhist priests began to try to influence the imperial court and interfere in politics. So when the imperial court decided to move the capital city from Nara to Heian, present-day Kyoto, it did not allow the temples to move. The court wanted to be free from Buddhist priests who had caused trouble.

Once the new capital was established, Emperor Kammu found two devout priests who he trusted to establish Buddhist centers in Kyoto: Saicho and Kukai. Saicho won approval to establish the Tendai sect on Mt. Hiei and Kukai won approval to establish the Shingon sect on Mt. Koya. These two priests led Buddhism in the Heian period.

◧ How did Buddhism first become associated with death and funerals?

In Shinto tradition, death and corpses were impurities. Any contact with either required purification. However, Buddhism offered a way to eliminate the impurities that the Japanese associated with death. With incantations and rituals performed by priests, Buddhism was able to transform the spirits of the dead. It could lead these spirits to enlightenment—even after death. If the living prayed for the soul of the deceased, that person could eventually become a Buddha.

The connection between Buddhism and funerals began early. As early as 685, the imperial court ordered that every aristocratic household should have a *butsudan*, a family Buddhist altar. The families were supposed to use the altar to worship their ancestors. The first cremation in Japan was that of a monk. It took place in 700, and before long the practice of cremation spread within the imperial court and the noble families. Later the customs of cremation and family altars spread to other parts of society. Families called on the Buddhist priests to carry out the rituals that removed the impurities that surrounded death.

The cremation rate in Japan is close to 99%.

◼ What is "the afterlife" like in Buddhism?

Buddhism holds that there are Six Realms of Existence (*Rokudo*). A person is reincarnated and reborn repeatedly in the cycle of these realms. The only way to escape this cycle is to gain enlightenment.

Those who have done evil are reborn in one of the hells. The ruler of hell is Emma, a frightening judge, who reviews each person's life and sends him to an appropriate hell. There are 8 great hells and 16 lesser hells. Those who have achieved enlightenment are reborn in the Pure Land of Amida Buddha.

Few Japanese today actually believe in the afterlife.

◼ What is *mappo*?

In the late Heian period (794–1185) Japanese entered a period of anxiety. One possible reason for this was the increase in the belief that there were three periods of the Buddhist dharma or law. According to this, the first period was the first 1,000 years after the Buddha lived on earth. In this period, believers could achieve salvation by way of living teachers. In the second 1,000 years, believers could achieve salvation by understanding the sutras. In the third 1,000 years the only hope for salvation was through faith in the teachings of the Pure Land.

Buddhist scholars estimated that the third period, called *mappo* or "the latter days of the Buddhist law," began in about 1052. Against this background, the creators of Kamakura Buddhism developed new ideas of how humans could achieve salvation.

◼ What are sutras (*okyo*)?

Sutras, *okyo*, are the teachings of Buddha. They were probably compiled around 2,000 years ago, which is some four centuries after Shakyamuni entered extinction. Sutras are not the direct teachings of the Buddha, but they contain the essence of his teachings. This was passed down by oral tradition through his disciples.

The *Heart Sutra* (*Hannya Shin-gyo*) is one of the most popular. The *Lotus Sutra* (*Hoke-kyo*) is the most influential sutra in Japanese culture. It says that the Buddha watches over and protects the living. It also says that everyone can become a Buddha.

◾ What is Zen?

Zen was brought to Japan beginning in the 13th century. It was brought by Eisai, who founded the Rinzai sect, and Dogen, who founded the Soto sect. These sects differ in the details, but they agree in stressing the importance of seated meditation. Japanese Zen Buddhism stresses monastic discipline. This includes living and practicing in a community under the guidance of a teacher who has gained enlightenment.

◾ Who was Kukai?

Kukai (774–835) and the older Saicho (767–822) are the two superstars of early Japanese Buddhism. Kukai was born in Shikoku and went to Kyoto to study Confucian, Taoist and Buddhist teachings. Eventually he entered the Buddhist priesthood.

He was given the opportunity to study Buddhism in T'ang China. He studied Esoteric Buddhism for three years under the master Hui-kuo. Kukai showed exceptional talent, and his master taught him the ultimate Esoteric teachings. Kukai returned to Japan with a great number of sutras, images and implements necessary for carrying out ceremonies.

Upon his return, he founded Shingon or Esoteric Buddhism in Japan and won the support of the emperor. He was given permission to establish a monastery for Shingon studies on Mt. Koya called Kongobuji. In addition, he was entrusted with the great Toji temple in Kyoto.

When he died, the emperor gave him the posthumous title Kobo Daishi, "great teacher who spread the teachings." In addition to his impressive documented accomplishments, a cult developed around him. He is credited with creating the *kana* syllabary, building important dams, sculpting famous images of Buddha, writing famous poems and originating the Shikoku pilgrimage of 88 temples.

◼ What is the Shingon sect?

Founded by Kukai, the Shingon sect is a form of Esoteric Buddhism or *Mikkyo*. The term *mikkyo* refers to "hidden teachings." According to Shingon, the early Buddhism that reached Japan was simplified so that ordinary believers could understand. The Shingon sect says that the true Buddha is Dainichi Nyorai (Maha Vairocana), whose teachings are not easily understood by ordinary believers.

The distinctive teaching of Shingon Buddhism is that a person can become a buddha in his or her own body. This teaching is called *sokushin jobutsu*. To reach this stage, a person uses mudras, mantras and mandalas in order to communicate with the Buddha. The Womb Realm Mandala and the Diamond Realm Mandala together form a visual representation of the entire universe. These visual, verbal and physical methods were considered more important than written scripture.

▣ Who was Saicho?

Saicho (767–822) became a Buddhist priest in Nara. But he became dissatisfied with the priests of the temples, who seemed to be concerned only with ceremonies for the government. He left Nara and built a hut on Mt. Hiei, northeast of Kyoto, where he could study, practice and learn how to spread the true teachings of Buddhism.

When Emperor Kammu moved the capital to Kyoto, he learned about this devoted priest named Saicho. Kammu supported Saicho and sent him to China in 804 to study Buddhism intensively. Saicho collected Buddhist works and received instruction in T'ien-t'ai teachings. When he returned, he began lecturing on the *Lotus Sutra* and was eventually able to establish a major center for the study of what in Japan came to be called Tendai Buddhism. This center was built on Mt. Hiei.

◼ What is the Tendai sect?

The Tendai sect of Buddhism was founded in 806 by Saicho. It is the Japanese counterpart of the Chinese T'ien-t'ai sect. Together with the Shingon sect, it was a dominant sect of Japanese Buddhism during the Heian period (794–1185).

Tendai is based on the Mahayana teaching of emptiness—all things are impermanent and devoid of existence. Prior to Saicho, Nara Buddhism said there is a class of beings who are not capable of attaining enlightenment. In contrast to this elitist view, Saicho taught that *all* sentient beings are capable of enlightenment.

His belief that everyone has buddha-nature became highly influential in all forms of Japanese Buddhism. Saicho also said that Tendai priests should help to save others as a way to save themselves. The priests should become bodhisattvas by living according to Mahayana teachings.

The Tendai sect is important because the founders of the major sects of the Kamakura period began their studies on Mt. Hiei.

◼ Who was Honen?

As a young man, Honen (1133–1212) was sent to Mt. Hiei to study Tendai Buddhism, but he remained discontented with what he learned. Honen believed that he could reach enlightenment through his own powers, but he was unsuccessful. Then he found a commentary that taught a new truth. It said that ordinary beings do not have the ability to attain enlightenment on their own. He then understood that the best way was to rely completely on Amida.

Honen left Mt. Hiei and began teaching "the exclusive practice of the *nembutsu*," invoking the name of the Buddha Amida. He gave up the idea that one had to be a priest in order to gain salvation. He preached his message without the permission of the government. Honen's actions challenged the older Nara schools, the Mt. Hiei priests, and the government. They had him banished because they saw his insistence on this "exclusive practice" as a threat. However, his teachings greatly appealed to ordinary people and he drew a significant following.

◼ What is the Jodo Sect?

The Jodo Sect of Pure Land Buddhism was founded by Honen. It is known for preaching the *nembutsu* (the phrase "*Namu Amida Butsu*" which means "I believe in the Buddha Amida") in order to gain rebirth in the Pure Land in the West.

The Jodo Sect sees Amida as a Buddha of

compassion, who created the Pure Land through the accumulation of merit and power over aeons. Amida made a series of 48 vows. The most important is the promise of rebirth within his realm to anyone who calls Amida's name ten times at death. This is his compassionate promise to all human beings.

◼ Who was Shinran?

As a disciple of Honen, Shinran (1173–1263) was also banished from the capital for preaching the exclusive practice of the *nembutsu*. Like Honen, he was later pardoned. But after Honen's death, Shinran found other Honen disciples preaching their own interpretations of the *nembutsu*. Shinran attempted to preach his teacher's "true teaching," and this became the Jodo Shin Sect, or "true essence of Pure Land Buddhism."

◼ What is the Jodo Shin Sect?

Shinran followed Honen in saying that wisdom is not reached by the effort of the self, *jiriki*. He believed that wisdom comes from the powers of Amida's vow. One should trust completely in the powers of Amida Buddha, *tariki*. The main difference with the Jodo Sect is that the Jodo Shin Sect says that we are already saved because Amida vowed to save us. Therefore, we merely recite the *nembutsu* as an act of thankfulness.

◼ Who was Nichiren?

Nichiren (1222–82) was born in Awa province, in present-day Chiba prefecture. As a child he decided to become a priest. He went to Kyoto to study at Mt. Hiei, before once again returning to Awa province.

As a result of his studies, he became convinced that the *Lotus Sutra* was the only true teaching. He denied the truth of all other teachings. This made other sects angry and he was forced to carry out his teachings elsewhere. He selected Kamakura, location of the *bakufu*, the military government.

A series of natural disasters, epidemics and famines occurred. They were followed by the threat of invasion of the country by the Mongol leader Kublai Khan. These events convinced Nichiren that the Japanese could only be saved if they embraced the *Lotus Sutra*. Nichiren announced his ideas to the government in *Treatise on the Establishment of the True Dharma and the Peace of the Nation (Rissho Ankokuron)*. He was banished to Izu and later to Sado for what he believed.

Nichiren's attacks on the other sects, his aggressive behavior and the arming of his followers brought persecution. But his fusion of old and new Buddhism filled a need among the warriors of Kamakura. They saw him as a master, similar in many ways to their military leaders.

◾ What is the Nichiren Sect?

While Honen and Shinran advocated the *nembutsu*, Nichiren promoted the chanting of the title (*daimoku*) of the name of the *Lotus Sutra: "Namu Myoho Renge-kyo" ("I believe in the Lotus Sutra").*

◾ Who was Ippen?

Ippen (1239–89), at the age of ten, decided to become a priest. He studied Tendai teachings at Enryakuji on Mt. Hiei. But his studies left him unfulfilled. He traveled to Kyushu where he became a devout Pure Land Buddhist. It is generally thought that Ippen gave up being a priest, took a wife, and then became a priest again in 1271.

Ippen combined Pure Land teachings with Shingon and folk elements of Shinto. Becoming known as a "wayfaring saint" (*yugyo shonin*), Ippen preached the importance of reciting Amida's name (*Namu Amida Butsu*) as the path to salvation. During his travels, he handed out pieces of paper that read: "Believe in Amida Buddha. Definite rebirth.

Six hundred thousand believers."

His uniqueness lies in his preaching the "dancing *nembutsu*," ecstatic dancing and preaching that won him a popular following. In contrast with Shinran, Ippen stressed the ecstatic incantation of Amida's name with complete abandonment. He believed in relying totally on the Buddha for salvation. Ippen founded the Ji Sect of Pure Land Buddhism.

◼ Who was Eisai?

Eisai (1141–1215) began studying Buddhist teachings at the age of seven. He became a Tendai monk at Enryakuji, but he became disillusioned by the loose way of life on Mt. Hiei. He traveled to China in 1168, and visited Tendai (T'ien-t'ai) monasteries and collected Tendai sutras. In 1187 he traveled to China a second time. He studied Zen under a Rinzai master who combined meditation, *koan* study and esoteric practices.

The *koan* are problems that seem illogical. They help the priest realize enlightenment intuitively—not by using logic.

Eisai returned to Japan in 1191. He taught Zen teachings in Kyushu and Kyoto, and this angered Tendai monks. In *The Propagation of Zen for the Protection of the Nation (Kozen gokoku-ron)*, he argued that Zen practice would give new energy to Tendai teachings and contribute to the security and welfare of the nation. This did not stop the attacks of the Tendai establishment.

He left Kyoto in 1198 and went to Kamakura. He received support from the Kamakura shogunate, which was looking for new cultural elements to strengthen its powers. He was welcomed and in 1202 was made founder and abbot of the Kenninji monastery, where he taught esoteric Buddhism, Tendai teachings and Zen.

◼ Who was Dogen?

Dogen (1200–53) studied Tendai teachings on Mt. Hiei and Rinzai teachings under Eisai's disciple Myozen. He traveled to China in 1223. There he studied under the master of the Chan (Soto Zen) school, Chang-weng Ju-ching. Within two months, Dogen achieved enlightenment and was recognized by his master as the successor to the tradition of Soto Zen.

Returning to Japan in 1227, he advocated single-minded devotion to Zen and thereby provoked the Tendai monks of the capital city. He then began writing his masterpiece *Treasury of the True Dharma Eye (Shobogenzo)*. In it he wrote that all people possess the potential to become a Buddha. He said that enlightenment is possible for anyone, if they just meditate in the lotus position. He called this *shikan taza*. He tried to get approval from the imperial court to teach Zen. But the Tendai leaders chased him from his temple.

He established a monastery in the mountains far away from Kyoto and Mt. Hiei priests. Dogen selected Echizen (present-day Fukui prefecture) as the site for a temple to train Soto sect monks. This temple, Eiheiji, continues to be a major Zen training institution known for its rigorous discipline.

◼ What are the main kinds of Buddhist deities?

In the worship hall of a temple and in mandalas, there is often more than one image. In many cases, a central image is surrounded by groups of other types of images. There are four basic kinds of Buddhist deities.

Nyorai (Buddha, Tathagata) are at the top of the hierarchy. In descending order, the most popular are Amida (the Buddha of Light), Yakushi (the Buddha of healing),

Nyorai

Bosatsu

Myoo

Tembu

Dainichi (the great sun Buddha, the cosmic Buddha), Birushana (Vairocana) and Shaka (the historical Buddha). You can recognize Yakushi Nyorai because he is usually surrounded by small Nyorai images. The Great Buddha at Todaiji in Nara is Birushana and the Great Buddha at Kamakura is Amida.

These Buddhas usually wear plain clothing like a monk would wear, have a shaved head, and wear no accessories. They may have particular symbolic marks on their bodies and be making a symbolic mudra (*inzo*) with their hands.

Bosatsu (Bodhisattva) are the second group from

Nyorai   Shaka   Bosatsu

the top. These are beings of great spiritual achievement who will one day become a Buddha. They have "postponed" becoming a Buddha until they have helped others reach Buddhahood. That is why they are seen as compassionate and why they are very popular among believers. This group includes Kannon, Jizo, Monju and Miroku. Miroku is designated to be the next Buddha, but this will not be anytime soon. This will not occur until 5,670,000,000 years after the Shakyamuni's enlightenment. Because the Buddha was enlightened about 2,600 years ago, Miroku still has a long time to wait.

Myoo

Tembu

These bodhisattvas very often have a gentle expression showing their compassion for all human beings. They often have long hair; wear bracelets, necklaces, and earrings; and hold various items in their hands.

Myoo are the third from the top. They are kings of wisdom and light and were originally Hindu deities. They were adopted into Esoteric Buddhism as incarnations of the cosmic Buddha. They save nonbelievers with the power of sacred words. The most common in this group is Fudo Myoo, whose cult is centered at Shinshoji (Narita-san) in Chiba prefecture.

They often have flaming hair, look fierce, bear weapons, and are surrounded by flames.

Tembu are the bottom of the pyramid. They are heavenly beings or deva. This group includes other deities adopted from Hindu. Each has its own powers and some have become objects of local cults. The most popular of this group are the pair Bonten and Taishakuten (seen at Todaiji and Toji); Nio or Kongo-rikishi (seen at Todaiji); the Shitenno or "Four Heavenly Kings" (seen at Horyuji and Toji); the feminine deities Benzaiten, Benten or Kisshoten; the Juni Shinsho or "Twelve Heavenly Generals"; and Daikokuten.

All these deities may have fierce features.

A fifth group includes *rakan* (arhats), who are Buddhists of high spiritual attainment. Certain temples have statues of 500 arhats, called *gohyaku rakan*. They tend to have unique, somewhat comical expressions. Also in this group are various eminent priests, scholars of Buddhism and patriarchs of various schools and sects.

Rakan

◼ Why does the Buddha have curly hair and big ears?

The spiral curls on the head of statues of the Buddha are called *rahotsu* or *rahatsu*. It is a symbol of enlightenment.

Statues with earrings are bodhisattvas, not buddhas. When Buddha gained enlightenment, he took off his earrings, leaving holes in his ears. The exceptionally large ears are a symbol of his preparation to hear the prayers of all believers.

◼ Why do Buddhist statues have a mole in the middle of the brow?

It looks like a mole, but this is called *byakugo* and it represents a curl of long white hair. It is one of the 32 physical features that Buddha is thought to possess. In many statues it is represented by a precious stone.

Byakugo   Rahotsu

■ What is Fudo Myoo?

Fudo Myoo, the Immovable King, symbolizes the necessity of being stern with some types of people, but also being compassionate. His fierce expression symbolizes his strong hostility to the enemies of Buddha's truth. His left eye is half-open; his right eye is staring. One eye looks up; the other looks down. Often he has a third eye in the middle of his forehead. Fangs stick out of his mouth. In one hand he has a sword, symbolizing compassion not violence. In the other, he has a lasso, to entangle passions. In Japan, he is said to ensure safety on the highway. Some Japanese purchase stickers of the frightening figure surrounded with flames as protection for their automobiles.

■ Why is Jizo so popular?

Bodhisattva, *bosatsu*, are not buddhas, but they have the full power to become buddhas. Jizo pledged not to become a Buddha, but instead to remain in the

Fudo Myoo   Jizo

human world to help people. Because of this, he has been popular in Japan since the Heian period, especially among the common people.

Jizo is usually shown as a monk, holding a jewel in the left hand and a staff in the right hand. He is regarded as the protector of travelers and children and helps them cross *Sanzu no kawa*, similar to the River Styx, in order to reach Paradise. Memorial services for miscarried or aborted fetuses (*mizuko kuyo*) often invoke Jizo, asking for protection of the *mizuko*, literally "water child."

◼ Why is Kannon so popular?

Like Jizo, Kannon is also a bodhisattva (*bosatsu*). Kannon has unlimited compassion for people in danger, protects people in this life and helps transport believers after death to the Pure Land.

Kannon was originally male, but in female form became popular as a protector of women giving birth.

Various representations of Kannon include the Horse-headed (*Bato*) Kannon, the Eleven-headed (*Juichi-men*) Kannon, the White-robed (*Byakue*) Kannon, and the Thousand-armed (*Senju*) Kannon. The so-called

Kannon

"Thousand-armed Kannon" actually have between 16 and 42 arms, symbolizing Kannon's infinite compassion. Each arm symbolizes the salvation of 25 worlds, so 40 arms represents the salvation of 1,000 worlds.

◼ What is an *asura*?

Ashura (*Asura*), origi-nally Hindu gods, were actually demon-gods or avatars. They were known as courageous

Asura

fighters. In Japanese Buddhism, the *asura* use their fierce fighting spirit to protect Buddhism. Kofukuji has a famous statue of an *asura* with six arms.

▣ What is a *daruma*?

A *daruma* is a figure with rounded head and body, with two large spaces for eyes. These figures represent Bodhidharma, the Indian priest who founded Zen Buddhism in China. It is said he spent nine years meditating in a cave and lost the use of his arms and legs. The round figures of Bodhidharma are weighted so that when you tip one over, it will roll upright on its own. This symbolizes the ability to recover from difficulties, so *daruma* are considered good luck charms.

Daruma figures are usually made of papier-mache and painted red. They are used as charms for fulfilling a wish, especially success in a public election or a successful harvest. Usually the eyes are not painted in when you buy it. You paint in one eye when you make your wish, then put it in the family shrine. When the wish is fulfilled, you paint in the other eye.

On March 3rd and 4th, a market selling *daruma* figures is held at Jindaiji in Mitaka (Tokyo).

▣ What makes a statue a *daibutsu*?

A *daibutsu*, "great Buddha," is about 5 meters or

16 feet tall. There are two famous "great Buddha" statues in Japan. The Kamakura Daibutsu dates from the mid-13th century. It is 11.4 meters (37.4 feet) tall. It was once inside a temple building, but that building was lost in 1495 to flood and earthquake. Since then, it has been out in the open. The Nara Daibutsu is an image of Buddha Vairocana at Todaiji. It is 15 meters (49.2 feet) high. The original was completed in 752, and it was considered the most splendid Buddhist statue in Japan. The current image has been restored several times.

◼ What defines a temple?

Called *tera* or *jiin* in Japanese, Buddhist temples are places where priests or nuns usually live and ceremonies take place. At the entrance to a temple there is usually a wooden gate with a tile roof.

The grounds of a temple usually contain a pagoda (*to*), a main hall (*kondo*, *hondo*), lecture hall (*kodo*), a bell tower (*shoro*, *shuro*), and a sutra repository (*kyozo*). If there are resident priests or nuns, there is also a dormitory (*sobo*) and dining hall (*jikido*). The main hall usually has one or more images of Buddha. There may be other deities surrounding the main images.

Although Buddhism and Shintoism were officially

separated during the Meiji period, you will some-times see a shrine on the grounds of a temple. You may also see Shinto deities protecting the Buddhas.

◨ What is a pagoda?

Pagodas (*to*) are built to store relics of the Buddha. The Japanese pagoda derives from the ancient Indian stupa. The stupa was a major structure in the monasteries of Indian Buddhism. Not all are

Temple Compound

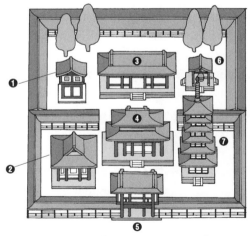

① dormitory   ④ main hall   ⑥ bell tower
② sutra repository   ⑤ gate   ⑦ pagoda
③ lecture hall

the commonly seen five-story pagodas (*goju-no-to*), but odd numbers of stories are definitely preferred.

They are constructed with a central pillar (*shimbashira*) surrounded by four inner pillars (*gawabashira*). The roofs curve upward and grow smaller as they move toward the top. The ends of the roofs usually have wind-bells (*futaku*). The finial (*sorin*) on the top has sacred rings (*horin*), topped by a "water flame" ornament (*suien*), a "dragon wheel" ornament (*ryusha*), and a "sacred jewel" ornament (*hoju*) at the very top.

Some pagodas in Japan do not have actual relics of the historical Buddha. Instead they have sutras or sacred ritual implements. The pagoda at Senso-ji has actual relics received from a temple in Sri Lanka.

▣ Why do priests shave their heads?

One story says that when the Buddha left his family's palace, he cut off his hair and vowed to seek the truth of existence. This may or may not be true, but a Buddhist priest shaves his head to remove any personal adornment and to distinguish himself from believers of other religions.

◾ Why do priests carry prayer beads?

Buddhist priests carry a string of beads called *juzu*, similar to a Catholic rosary. Priests place the *juzu* over their hands when they worship. They also use these beads for counting *nembutsu*.

Usually there are 108 beads, one for each of the 108 illusions or earthly passions. There are also strings with fractions of this number, including 54, 36, 27, and 18. The beads may be made of crystal or wood. This string of beads is a typical symbol of Buddhist faith.

◾ How does a temple receive income?

Basically, temples depend on donations for income. Some donations come from the parishioners, *danka*, for whom the priest says prayers and carries out ceremonies. Consequently, carrying out funeral ceremonies and the series of memorial ceremonies is an important source. Most families ask a priest to offer prayers and chant a sutra seven days after death, and every seven days until the 49th day. This results in a donation to the priest which goes to the support of the temple.

Some temples have income from the sale of amulets and talismans. Some temples operate kindergartens. Large, popular temples may charge admission for sightseeing purposes.

On a rare occasion, you may see a monk begging for alms. Usually the monk will wear a woven straw hat and hold an alms bowl, while chanting a sutra.

▣ What is the role of *danka*?

A *danka* is a family that is affiliated to a particular temple of a Buddhist sect. The family requests the priest of that temple to perform funeral and memorial services. In return, the family makes donations to support the temple.

During the Edo period, the *bakufu* (military government) ordered resident families of each local neighborhood to become "members" of a local temple. This was done to make sure that people would not practice Christianity, which was banned. In this sense, Buddhist temples served as a way of registering citizens and controlling them. Today, *danka* families usually continue the family tradition of belonging to a certain temple without really knowing or caring about the specific teachings of the sect.

▣ What animal symbols appear in Buddhism iconography?

The phoenix is a mythological bird introduced from China. It was believed to appear when the ruler of a nation was righteous. Among the most famous are the phoenix on top of Kinkakuji (Kyoto) and the Phoenix Hall at Byodoin (Uji, near Kyoto).

The *kirin* was also thought to appear when the ruler of a country was righteous. It resembles a cross between a giraffe and a fiery horse.

phoenix

The dragon symbolized the emperor in China. In Japan, it symbolizes the will and power of heaven.

The birth of Buddha is connected with a white elephant, so that animal

kirin

white elephant

dragon

appears in iconography.

The peacock is supposedly able to eat symbolic poisons including fear, passions and suffering.

peacock

◼ What are *senja fuda*?

Senja fuda are traditional stickers with the name of a pilgrim visiting a temple. In the past, people put these on the gates or pillars of temples to show that they had made a pilgrimage to the site. They hoped to gain merit for doing so. Nowadays temples discourage the practice because it damages the surface of the wood and detracts from the appearance of the temple.

◼ How does one worship at a temple?

Unlike at a shrine, you quietly place your palms together in prayer rather than clapping. The *kami* need to be summoned, but the buddhas are always present and waiting.

◼ What is a *goma* ceremony?

The *goma* ceremony, or "fire ceremony," comes from Esoteric Buddhism. The Japanese word *goma* means "to burn." In the ceremony, fire symbolizes the wisdom of the Buddha, and is used to burn away illusion and worldly desires, the sources of human suffering.

In the ceremony, the priest burns *goma* wood in the center of a platform set up in front of an image of Kobo Daishi. Prayers are offered particularly for those who have reached critical years of their lives. The fire destroys all calamities, and prayers bring safety and good fortune to the participants.

The temples on Mt. Koya hold *goma* rituals every morning. Nearer to Tokyo, Kawasaki Daishi temple, also called Heikenji, is well known for its *goma* ceremony.

■ What is the meaning of "*Namu Amida Butsu*"?

The chant "*Namu Amida Butsu*" means "I believe in Amida Buddha." It is chanted in the hope of being reborn in the Pure Land of Amida.

The practice was popularized by Honen in the 12th century. He taught that just saying this was the best path to salvation.

■ What is the meaning of "*Myoho Renge-kyo*"?

The chant "*Namu Myoho Renge-kyo*" means "I believe in the Lotus Sutra." It is the *daimoku* or mantra of the Nichiren sect of Buddhism.

◼ Why do Buddhists cremate and put the remains in a grave?

Before Buddhism arrived, the Japanese buried the dead. They believed that the dead would return to life and cause problems for the living. Therefore, they wanted to be sure the body could not rise up again.

When Buddhism arrived, the founder of the Hosso sect, named Dosho, requested that his body be cremated. He is thought to be the first person cremated in Japan.

The Japanese eventually combined the custom of cremation with the setting up of a monument covering the remains. In the beginning only the elite did this, but beginning in the Edo period the custom spread to ordinary people. Currently, 99% of the deceased are cremated and ashes are placed in a funerary urn. Most urns are placed in the family tomb, with those of earlier generations or other family members. Because land is hard to find, there are now vertical mausolea where the ashes of large numbers of people can be kept.

◼ How many memorial services, *hoji*, are held after death?

The Buddhist custom that came from India was

to hold seven memorial services. These were held between the seventh and forty-ninth days after death. Chinese Buddhists added a service on the 100th day, the first anniversary and the third anniversary. Japanese Buddhists added services on the 13th, 17th, 23rd and 33rd anniversaries.

◼ What is a *butsudan*?

A *butsudan* is a small cabinet containing an image of Buddha and memorial tablets, *ihai*, for the family ancestors. Generally, the cabinet has candles, an incense burner, a bell and a small scroll or statue. Some families also put a photograph of the departed. Often the family makes an offering of rice and water, lights incense and a candle, rings the small bell and places the palms of the hands together in prayer in what is called *gassho*.

◼ What is a memorial tablet?

A memorial tablet, *ihai*, has the posthumous Buddhist name of the deceased person written on it. Depending on the sect, it may also have Sanskrit characters, the name of the sect or the name of the temple. Generally, for the first 49 days following death, the tablet is plain wood. After that period has passed, a new one is made which is often painted or varnished black. It is kept in the Buddhist altar in the home.

◼ Why are the dead given Buddhist names?

Originally, the *kaimyo*, an ordination name, was a name given to a person when he or she became a Buddhist priest. It showed that the person has faith in the teachings of Buddha and promised to follow them. Japanese Buddhism says that everyone has the potential for becoming a buddha. But not everyone becomes a priest. So people are given this kind of ordination name after death.

◼ What is a *sotoba*?

These narrow wooden planks (*sotoba*) are placed at graves. On the front is written a posthumous Buddhist name or a scripture. The characters are written in Sanskrit, one of the sacred languages used to transmit Buddhism to Japan. On the back may be written the name of the donor.

These planks range from one to two meters in length and are placed upright at the tomb. The tomb itself is for the whole family, but the *sotoba* is offered for the repose of the deceased individual. The shape of each *sotoba*, from the bottom, has five divisions, representing the five elements: earth, water, fire, wind and air. One type of traditional gravestone has the same five divisions.

◉ What is a mandala?

Mandala, *mandara*, are paintings that represent the Buddhist universe. They make complex ideas easier to grasp by making these ideas visual. They are symmetrical symbolic cosmologies that usually show the relations between four kinds of images: buddhas, bodhisattvas, myoo and tembu. The two main mandalas are the Diamond (Kongo-kai) and the Womb (Taizo-kai) mandalas. The Shingon sect has rituals showing the dynamic relationships between these two mandalas.

In addition to the two-dimensional mandala paintings, there is another variety. The statues of the Buddhas in a worship hall may form a mandala, particularly in Esoteric Buddhism.

Shinto also has mandalas, some of which are combinations of Shinto and Buddhism. The most famous is found in three shrines of Kumano. Other Shinto mandalas show a bird's-eye view of a shrine in its natural setting.

◾ What happens at *O-bon*?

O-bon, the Bon Festival, is the most important annual event of the Buddhist calendar. It is the Buddhist Festival of the Dead and it lasts from the 12th through the 16th of August. The traditional period, still observed in some regions, is July 12th through 16th.

Families prepare an altar called a *bon-dana*. This is for the spirits of the ancestors to stay during the festival. On the altar are placed small figures of cows and horses made of cucumbers and eggplants with legs made from toothpicks. These symbolize the animals that carry the spirits. The family may also place flowers, fresh fruit, incense and candles on the altar.

On the evening of August 12, families may light a small fire at the door of their home in order to welcome back the souls of the departed. These small fires are called *mukaebi*. In some regions, a special paper lantern is lit instead. August 13th is the actual day of *O-bon*. A similar fire is lit on August 16th to send the souls off, and this is called *okuribi*. The Gozan no Okuribi in Kyoto is a famous example of this custom.

▣ What is the *okuribi* of the Gozan in Kyoto?

Okuribi ("sending off fires") are ceremonial fires that are lit on the evening of the last day of *O-bon*. They are supposed to send the spirits of the dead on their way back to the underworld.

On August 16, the Gozan Farewell Bonfire (*Gozan no okuribi*) is held in Kyoto. On mountains around the city, bonfires shaped like Chinese characters are lit to guide the spirits of the dead. They are two bonfires with the character for "great" (*dai*), one with the two characters "*Myoho*" (the name of a Buddhist sutra), and one each with the shapes of a ship (to carry the ancestors back) and a *torii*. The tradition of this bonfire dates back to the Muromachi period.

▣ What is *higan*?

This twice-a-year celebration is special to Japanese Buddhism. The weeklong periods called *higan* center on the spring equinox and the autumn equinox. *Higan* includes the equinox, the three days before it and the three days after it. During these two periods, Buddhist services are performed. Families visit the family grave, *haka mairi*, during these periods to pay their respects to their ancestors.

The word *higan* in Buddhism means "the other shore," or Nirvana.

◼ What is *haka mairi*?

At *higan*, *O-bon* and other times through the year, family members visit the graves of their ancestors. They bring water in a bucket to clean the tombstone. They weed around it and pick up any trash they find. Then they offer flowers and incense and offer a prayer.

◼ What is *hana matsuri*?

Hana Matsuri, the Flower Festival, celebrates the birthday of the Buddha. It is held every year on April 8. A small altar decorated with flowers (*hanami-do*) is created. On it is placed a statue of Buddha as a child. This figure points one hand toward heaven and the other toward earth. This symbolizes that he is honored in both places. People pour water or sweet tea (*amacha*) on the statue to honor him. This tradition comes from the story that at Buddha's birth, dragons descended from heaven and poured scented water on him. *Hana Matsuri* is also called *kanbutsu-e*.

◼ Why do people undertake the Shikoku 88-temple pilgrimage?

The "Shikoku pilgrimage," *Shikoku henro* or *Shikoku hachijuhakkasho*, is a route that links 88 specific places of worship. There is no clear explanation of how this pilgrimage developed. However, the places are believed to have some connection with Kukai, also known as Kobo Daishi. Kukai was born in Zentsuji, in Shikoku, and after studying in China, he established Shingon Buddhism on Mt. Koya. His "home ground" was Shikoku, so it is not surprising that a cult devoted to him developed there.

The pilgrimage, which circles the island of Shikoku, is 1,400 kilometers (870 miles) long. It includes eighty Shingon temples and eight temples of other sects. In good weather—spring is most common—it takes six weeks to walk the entire route. The usual route is clockwise. However, one is free to go counter-clockwise, do it in sections, complete it all at one time, or spread it over a period of years. Large numbers of participants now travel the route by tour bus in ten to twelve days.

Traditional clothing includes a white shirt, a bamboo hat, and a wooden staff. The white shirt symbolizes the special condition of withdrawal from the everyday world. The staff symbolizes the spirit of Kobo Daishi which accompanies the pilgrim at all times. Some individuals travel alone, while others travel in large groups conducted by a leader called a *sendatsu*, who tells about each place and leads the worship at each location. At each temple, the pilgrim can have a priest put the temple's seal (*shuin*) in a special pilgrim's book called a *nokyocho*. The priest also adds some calligraphy in black ink.

Motivations for setting out on the pilgrimage vary widely, and the pilgrims are not necessarily followers of Shingon Buddhism. Some join for personal reasons, such as regaining health, reflecting on a failure, or seeking a path in life. In the 1990s, they increasingly included middle-aged men who had been "restructured" and were trying to find new meaning in their lives. Then again a large number are simply tourists. They want to enjoy a traditional natural setting with a historical, religious twist.

◼ Why do people ring temple bells 108 times on New Year's Eve?

Beginning on New Year's Eve, temple bells are rung to announce the passing of the old year and the coming of the new. Buddhists believe that there are 108 earthly desires or passions, *bonno*, and that by ringing the bell 108 times, one desire is dispelled each time. These "New Year's Eve bells" are called *joya no kane*.

CHAPTER 5

Christianity in Japan

Chapter 5
日本のキリスト教

　イエズス会を創設し、その修道士として知られていたフランシスコ・ザビエルはキリスト教を広めるため、二人の宣教師を連れて1549年に日本へやって来ました。

　ザビエルは九州の平戸を訪れ、京都へと向かいました。天皇に拝謁して日本全土に布教をする許しを得ようとしたものの、不首尾に終わります。ザビエルは1551年に日本を去ってインドへと向かい、その翌年に亡くなりました。

　ザビエルらの布教によりキリスト教信仰は九州に広まり、特に長崎近辺において最も成果を得ました。九州の大名にはキリスト教に改宗する者もおり、それに従うものたちが次々と入信しました。その動機の一部にあったのは、キリスト教を受け入れることで藩に他国との貿易の道筋をつけたいというものでした。

キーワード

☐ Amakusa Shiro 天草四郎
☐ Anjiro アンジロウ
☐ Francis Xavier フランシスコ・ザビエル
☐ kakure kirishitan 隠れキリシタン
☐ sakoku 鎖国
☐ Shimabara Rebellion 島原の乱
☐ Toyotomi Hideyoshi 豊臣秀吉

◾ Who brought Christianity to Japan and when?

Francis Xavier (1506–52) came to Japan with two priests in 1549 in order to spread Christianity. He was the founder of the Society of Jesus, also known as the Jesuits. While spreading Christianity in India and Malacca, he met a Japanese man named Anjiro. What Anjiro told Xavier about Japan encouraged him to go there to preach Christianity.

Xavier visited Hirado in Kyushu and traveled to Kyoto. He tried to meet the emperor to get permission to preach throughout Japan, but was unsuccessful. Xavier left Japan for India in 1551 and died the next year.

◾ Who accepted Christianity and why?

Xavier and his followers were most successful in spreading Christian belief in Kyushu, especially near Nagasaki. Some of the Kyushu daimyo converted to Christianity and their followers joined them. Part of the motivation for accepting Christianity was that the local governments hoped that it would lead to trade with other nations.

JAPANESE RELIGION

◼ Why was Christianity banned?

Toyotomi Hideyoshi was the first national leader to suppress Catholic Christianity. Under the Tokugawa shogunate, missionaries were banned from Japan and Christianity was banned from time to time.

Serious suppression began with the Shimabara Rebellion in the Shimabara peninsula near Nagasaki. The area suffered from continuous poverty, high taxes and continuing famine. A peasant rebellion broke out in 1637, and the peasant were joined by samurai who had no employment. They were led by a young leader named Amakusa Shiro and others, who happened to be Christians. The shogunate attacked the rebels and laid siege to Hara Castle where the remaining rebels fought desperately. In 1638 the rebels ran out of food, the castle was captured and all of the occupants were killed. After this defeat, Christianity in Japan virtually disappeared.

◼ What are "hidden Christians" (*kakure kirishitan*)?

After 1638, some Christians went underground, becoming "hidden Christians," *kakure kirishitan*. They practiced their beliefs in secret. They kept their beliefs and practices, while appearing to become

Buddhists. They had no priests, so they depended on lay leaders. They passed on by word of mouth the liturgy and doctrines they had learned from the foreign missionaries. This continued until the end of the Tokugawa period in 1868.

◼ When was Christianity permitted again?

Christianity continued to be banned until the end of the period of national seclusion, *sakoku*. During the last years of the Tokugawa period, Catholic missionaries were gradually allowed into Japan to resume activity. A Catholic church was built in the Oura section of Nagasaki in 1864. The next year a group of farmers from the village of Urakami visited the church. They announced to the priest, "Our hearts are the same as yours." This was the first evidence that so-called "hidden Christians" (*kakure kirishitan*), existed in Japan.

However, it was not until 1873 that the ban on Christianity was completely lifted.

◼ What impact has Christianity had on Japan?

Christian missions established private schools from elementary through university levels. The Catholics established the universities now called Sophia University (Tokyo) and Nanzan University (Nagoya).

Protestant groups established Doshisha University (Kyoto), Aoyama Gakuin University (Tokyo), Rikkyo University (Tokyo) and International Christian University (Tokyo). Few of the students at these universities are Christian, but they are exposed to Christian beliefs through chapel services and regular classes. According to Japanese government statistics, about 2.5% of the Japanese population is Christian.

◼ Why do some Japanese have Christian weddings?

One survey says that in 2018 about 55% of all weddings in Japan were "Christian" in style. This includes weddings at "chapels" in hotels where a person who is not a real "minister" performs the ceremonies. There is no marital counseling beforehand and the couple do not attend church.

The other weddings are almost all Shinto in form.

New Religions and New-New Religions

Chapter 6
新興宗教と新新興宗教

　戦後の混乱期に出現した新しい宗教は「新興宗教」と呼ばれるようになり、戦後憲法によって保障された信教の自由の下、その多くが大いに栄えました。新しい規定では宗教組織に完全な自治権が与えられ、政府の役割はそういった組織を正規の宗教団体として登録することのみでした。いったん正式に登録されるとそれらの団体は納税免除の対象となり、この恩恵によって次々と新興宗教が生まれました。

　多くの場合、カリスマ教祖というものも存在していました。奇跡が起こったり、魂が癒されたりすることもカリスマ教祖のおかげだと考えられている場合もあります。

　さらに新しくできた宗教団体は、時に「新新興宗教」と呼ばれます。

キーワード

- ☐ Agon-shu 阿含宗
- ☐ Byakko Shinkokai 白光真宏会
- ☐ Konko-kyo 金光教
- ☐ Kyoha Shinto 教派神道
- ☐ Omoto-kyo 大本（教）
- ☐ PL Kyodan PL（パーフェクトリバティー）教団
- ☐ Reiyukai 霊友会
- ☐ Rissho Koseikai 立正佼成会
- ☐ Seicho no ie 生長の家
- ☐ Soka Gakkai 創価学会
- ☐ Tenrikyo 天理教

◼ What are the so-called "New Religions"?

The new religions that appeared during the chaos that followed World War II came to be called *shinko shukyo*, "new religions." Many prospered under the freedom of religion guaranteed by the postwar constitution. Under the new regulations, religious bodies were given complete autonomy. The government's only role was to register them as legitimate religious bodies. Once properly registered, these groups were exempt from taxation, a benefit that promoted a lot of new religions.

Most of these groups was a combination of reverence for ancestors, promise of worldly benefits and focus on a particular sutra. For some groups, it was not necessary to have doctrines or even sacred scriptures but only to offer potential members some sort of benefit or the promise of salvation. Among the most common of the traditional scriptures that were reinterpreted was the *Lotus Sutra*, and many of the groups that embraced this sutra consisted exclusively of laypeople, that is, people with no connection to an ordained priesthood.

In the majority of cases, there was also a

charismatic or shamanistic leader, a person who is revered in a special way or a person whose life story in some way comes to symbolize the teachings of the organization. Miraculous powers and spiritual healing may also be attributed to these leaders.

Religious groups formed more recently are sometimes referred to as "New New Religions" (*shin-shinko shukyo*).

◼ What is Tenrikyo?

Literally "religion of divine wisdom," Tenrikyo is one of the largest religious groups in Japan. A Shinto sect (*Kyoha Shinto*), it was founded in a village in Nara Prefecture which is now Tenri City.

It promotes the idea that a better world is possible if people simply develop a pure and simple heart. Tenrikyo ethics hold that human beings are not evil, but their souls are covered with eight kinds of dust (*yatsu no hokori*): greed, stinginess, partiality, hatred, animosity, anger, covetousness and arrogance. It is these that cause human unhappiness and prevent human beings from "shining." If these forms of "dust" are removed, the human spirit will shine once more and salvation will be achieved.

Tenrikyo has expanded widely, and it now operates Tenri University, a hospital, a radio station and

Tenri Central Library, which contains a significant collection of National Treasures and Important Cultural Properties. Tenrikyo has some two million adherents and is expanding into Brazil, Congo and the United States.

◼ What is Konko-kyo?

Konko-kyo, literally "teaching of the golden light," is a syncretist sect of Shinto. The sect believes that all humans are equal and that if a person worships the deity Konjin sincerely, works industriously and is considerate of others, he or she will be blessed by the deity. As of 1990, the sect claimed some 450,000 members. Tenrikyo and Konkokyo are sometimes seen as the forerunners of the "new religions" that sprang up after the Second World War.

◼ What is Omoto-kyo?

Omoto-kyo, literally "teaching of the great origin," was established in 1892. It is the parent of a large number of separate religious organizations.

Omoto-kyo teachings criticized contemporary society and called for reform. Its message was that salvation began not with the elite but with the common people. This was an idea which seemed both revolutionary and menacing to the authority of the

Emperor and the government. While Omoto-kyo did not reject the imperial system, the organization was suppressed because it said that a *kami* other than the emperor would transform the world into one of peace and brotherhood. After World War II, Omoto-kyo membership declined significantly.

◼ What is PL Kyodan?

PL Kyodan, the Church of Perfect Liberty, was founded in 1946. The name comes from English: "Perfect Liberty." Based on the idea that "Life is Art," the group holds "the artistic life" as its ideal. Happiness and satisfaction will result when the individual expresses his or her personality perfectly in every way—in the interest of other people and society as a whole.

The organization's headquarters are in Tonda-bayashi, on the outskirts of Osaka. Surrounding this building are a golf course, a hospital, an elementary school, a middle school, a high school (PL Gakuen).

◼ What is Seicho no Ie?

Seicho no Ie, House of Growth, is a religious sect founded in 1929. It stresses man's relationship with the divine and the individual's efforts to realize "the truth of life." This realization promises happiness and victory over both illness and poverty. In its eclectic viewpoint, the teachings of Christianity, Buddhism, Shinto and all other true religions are actually one and the same. In line with this, members are free to become members of other religions, too. The group shows no resistance to other religions, unless that other group requires that people suffer. The sect is classified by the Japanese government among "other religions." Seicho no Ie has also stressed proselytizing overseas.

▣ What is Reiyukai?

Reiyukai, Spiritual-Friends-Association, is one of the largest lay religious organizations in Japan. The group has no direct affiliation with any Buddhist sect.

The teachings of Reiyukai stress veneration of ancestors, the family system and the Buddhist tradition based in the *Lotus Sutra*. Reiyukai originally saw veneration of ancestors and a revival of the extended family and traditional morality as the keys to social harmony. The possibility of salvation in this world was seen as grounded in faithful veneration of ancestral spirits. Among the important practices of the group is the group meeting called *hoza*, literally "Dharma circle," in which a lay leader counsels members on personal problems and offers religious instruction.

▣ What is Soka Gakkai?

Founded in 1930, Soka Gakkai is an independent lay organization of the Nichiren Shoshu sect of Buddhism. Its aims include a reform of society based on the teachings of Nichiren.

Assuming that all human beings possess buddha-nature, Soka Gakkai teaches that faith, practice and study are essentials. The first is the chanting of "*Namu Myoho Renge-kyo*" (I believe in the Lotus Sutra) and reciting the sutra. The second is including Buddhist activities into daily life, the key element of which is propagating the teachings of Nichiren Shoshu. Characteristic of this aspect is *shakubuku*, aggressive propagation. The third refers to studying the teachings of Nichiren. The sect claims that only Soka Gakkai and Nichiren Shoshu represent accurately the truth discovered by Nichiren. All religious activities outside this tradition are to be considered as heresy and are to be avoided. Members are not supposed to participate in any Shinto activities such as shrine visits at the New Year or in festivals.

Soka Gakkai has its own university (Soka University), daily newspaper (*Seikyo Shimbun*) and cultural and social programs. In 1964 it founded a full-fledged political party, Komeito (Clean Government Party), but separated from the party in 1970.

◼ What is Rissho Koseikai?

Rissho Koseikai (Society for the Establishment of Righteousness and Personal Perfection through Fellowship) is one of the largest organizations of lay Buddhists in Japan. Founded in 1938, it is one of the new religions based on Nichiren tradition and the *Lotus Sutra*, but it has no formal relation with a Nichiren sect.

It emphasizes making the *Lotus Sutra* easy for laypeople to understand, emphasizes the interdependence of all human beings and all things in the universe and therefore encourages the veneration of ancestors.

Among the central activities is participation in *hoza*, small groups aimed at self-reflection and personal counseling and instruction by a group leader. This method has proved effective in keeping members involved with one another and in attracting new members. Rissho Koseikai is also known for its ecumenical cooperation and promotion of world peace, especially through the Niwano Peace Prize, which is awarded to remarkable religious leaders or groups that contribute to dialogue between religions, protection of human rights and the resolution of conflict.

◼ What is Agon-shu?

This "new-new religion," founded in 1978, gathers considerable media attention as a result of its spectacular fire rites, *goma*. The group claims that unhappy spirits of the dead affect the living by causing spiritual hindrances and *tatari* (pollution). Through its fire rites, these afflicting spirits are believed to be transformed into benevolent spirits that bestow benefits on participants.

Its most well-known feature is its *hoshi matsuri*, or star festival, held annually outside Kyoto on February 11. That day happens to be National Foundation Day. Widely advertised in the media—and as a result attended by over half a million visitors—this outdoor ritual centers on the burning of two huge pyres of branches upon which are piled wooden sticks inscribed with requests are written. The occasion is carefully orchestrated to give attendees an opportunity to express their hopes for world peace, for happiness and the salvation of their ancestors.

◼ What is Byakko Shinkokai?

This group is best known for erecting "peace poles" that have the words "May Peace Prevail on Earth" written in the local language. The group incorporates prayers for the individual and for world peace in its rituals. It portrays Japan as the holy core from which peace will spread throughout the world.

Word List

・本文で使われている全ての語を掲載しています（LEVEL 1、2）。ただし、
　LEVEL 3 以上は、中学校レベルの語を含みません。

・語形が規則変化する語の見出しは原形で示しています。不規則変化語は本文
　中で使われている形になっています。

・一般的な意味を紹介していますので、一部の語で本文中で実際に使われている
　品詞や意味と合っていないことがあります。

・品詞は以下のように示しています。

名 名詞	代 代名詞	形 形容詞	副 副詞	動 動詞	助 助動詞
前 前置詞	接 接続詞	間 間投詞	冠 冠詞	略 略語	俗 俗語
頭 接頭語	尾 接尾語	記 記号	関 関係代名詞

A

☐ **abandonment** 名 放棄

☐ **abbot** 名 住職

☐ **ability** 名 できること、(～する) 能力

☐ **abolish** 動 廃止する、撤廃する

☐ **abort** 動 胎児を流産する、妊娠中絶する

☐ **abstain** 動 (～を) 控える、つつしむ

☐ **accept** 動 ①受け入れる ②同意する、認める

☐ **accessible** 形 近づきやすい、利用できる

☐ **accessory** 名 付属品、装飾品、アクセサリー

☐ **accompany** 動 ①ついていく、つきそう ②(～に) ともなって起こる

☐ **accomplishment** 名 ①完成、達成 ②業績

☐ **according** 副《– to ～》～によれば [よるど]

☐ **accumulation** 名 蓄積、集積

☐ **accurately** 副 正確に、正しく、きちんと

☐ **accuse** 動《– of ～》～ (の理由で) 告訴 [非難] する

☐ **achieve** 動 成し遂げる、達成する、成功を収める

☐ **achievement** 名 ①達成、成就 ②業績

☐ **act** 名 行為、行い

☐ **actively** 副 活発に、活動的に

☐ **activity** 名 活動、活気

☐ **actual** 形 実際の、現実の

☐ **actually** 副 実際に、本当に、実は

☐ **add** 動 加える、足す

☐ **addition** 名 付加、追加、添加 in addition 加えて、さらに

☐ **adherent** 名 信者

☐ **administration** 名 管理、統治、政権

☐ **administrator** 名 経営者、理事、管理者

☐ **admission** 名 入場料

☐ **adopt** 動 ①採択する、選ぶ ②承認する

☐ **adornment** 名 装飾品 personal adornments 装身具

☐ **advertise** 動 広告する、宣伝する

☐ **advocate** 動 主張する、提唱する

114

- □ **aeon** 图 永劫, 無限に長い年月
- □ **affair** 图《-s》業務, 仕事, やるべきこと **Agency of Cultural Affairs** 文化庁
- □ **affect** 動 影響する
- □ **affiliated** 形 提携している, 関連のある
- □ **affiliation** 图 所属, 提携
- □ **afflicting** 形 苦しめる, 悲惨な
- □ **after** 熟 name after ～にちなんで名付ける
- □ **afterlife** 图 死後の世界, あの世
- □ **afterworld** 图 死後の世界, 黄泉の国
- □ **agency** 图 機関, 政府機関 **Agency of Cultural Affairs** 文化庁
- □ **aggressive** 形 ①攻撃的な, 好戦的な ②活動的な ③強引な
- □ **aging** 图 老化, 高齢化
- □ **Agon-shu** 图 阿含宗
- □ **agriculture** 图 農業, 農耕
- □ **aim** 動 ねらう, 目指す
- □ **allow** 動 許す,《－…to～》…が～するのを可能にする, …に～させておく
- □ **alms** 图 施し物 **alms bowl** 托鉢の鉢
- □ **altar** 图 祭壇
- □ **although** 接 ～だけれども, ～にもかかわらず, たとえ～でも
- □ **amacha** 图 甘茶
- □ **Amakusa Shiro** 天草四郎《?– 1638, 江戸時代初期のキリシタンで, 島原の乱における一揆軍の最高指導者》
- □ **Amaterasu** 图 天照大御神(あまてらすおおみかみ)《日本神話に主神として登場する神。女神と解釈され, 高天原を統べる主宰神で, 皇祖神とされる》
- □ **amazing** 形 驚くべき, 見事な
- □ **Amida** 图 阿弥陀仏, 阿弥陀如来(あ

みだぶつ, あみだにょらい)《大乗仏教の如来の一つ》
- □ **among** 熟 be popular among ～の間で人気がある
- □ **amount** 图 量, 額
- □ **amulet** 图 お守り
- □ **ancestor** 图 祖先, 先祖
- □ **ancestral** 形 祖先の, 先祖代々の
- □ **ancient** 形 昔の, 古代の
- □ **anger** 图 怒り 動 怒る, ～を怒らせる
- □ **animosity** 图 敵意, 憎しみ, 対立
- □ **Anjiro** 图 アンジロウ《日本人で最初のキリシタン》
- □ **anniversary** 图 記念日, 記念祭
- □ **announce** 動 (人に)知らせる, 公表する
- □ **annual** 形 年1回の, 例年の, 年次の
- □ **annually** 副 毎年, 年1回
- □ **another** 熟 one another お互い
- □ **anti-Buddhist** 图 反仏教
- □ **anxiety** 图 心配, 不安
- □ **anyone** 代 ①《疑問文・条件節で》誰か ②《否定文で》誰も (～ない) ③《肯定文で》誰でも
- □ **anytime** 副 いつでも
- □ **anzan** 图 安産
- □ **Aoyama Gakuin University** 青山学院大学
- □ **appeal** 動 求める, 訴える
- □ **appear** 動 ①現れる, 見えてくる ②(～のように)見える, ～らしい **appear to** するように見える
- □ **appearance** 图 外見, 印象
- □ **appoint** 動 任命する, 指名する
- □ **appreciation** 图 感謝
- □ **approach** 動 ①接近する ②話を持ちかける
- □ **appropriate** 形 適切な, ふさわしい, 妥当な

A

B
C
D
E
F
G
H
I
J
K
L
M
N
O
P
Q
R
S
T
U
V
W
X
Y
Z

□ **approval** 图 承認, 認可

□ **argue** 動 ①論じる, 議論する ②主張する

□ **arhat** 图 阿羅漢《仏教において最高の悟りを得た聖者のこと》

□ **aristocratic** 形 貴族の

□ **arrogance** 图 横柄さ, 傲慢さ

□ **arrow** 图 矢, 矢のようなもの

□ **art** 熟 works of art 芸術作品

□ **artistic** 形 芸術的な, 芸術(家)の

□ **as** 熟 as a result その結果(として) as a result of ～の結果(として) as a whole 全体として as many as ～ もの数の be known as ～として知られている be regarded as ～と見なされる be seen as ～として見られる see ～ as … ～を…と考える such as ～ たとえば～, ～のような

□ **ascetic** 图 苦行者 形 苦行の ascetic practice 苦行

□ **ash** 图 ①灰, 燃えかす ②《-es》遺骨, なきがら

□ **Ashura** 图 阿修羅《仏教の守護神》

□ **Asia** 图 アジア

□ **aspect** 图 状況, 局面, 側面

□ **assist** 動 手伝う, 列席する, 援助する

□ **assistance** 图 援助, 支援

□ **associate** 動 ①連合[共同]する, 提携する ②～を連想する ③交際する

□ **association** 图 協会

□ **assume** 動 仮定する, 当然のことと思う

□ **Asura** 图 阿修羅《仏教の守護神》

□ **attach** 動 取り付ける, 添える

□ **attachment** 图 愛着

□ **attack** 動 襲う, 攻める

□ **attain** 動 達成する, 成し遂げる, 達する

□ **attainment** 图 ①到達, 達成 ②《-s》(達成して得た)学識

□ **attempt** 動 試みる, 企てる 图 試み, 企て, 努力

□ **attend** 動〔会合・パーティー・催し物など〕に出席[参加]する, 〔式典など〕に参列する

□ **attendee** 图 出席者

□ **attention** 图 注意, 集中

□ **attract** 動 ①引きつける, 引く ②魅力がある, 魅了する

□ **attribute** 動 起因すると考える, (～の)せいにする

□ **auspicious** 形 縁起のよい, 吉兆の

□ **authority** 图 権威, 権力, 権限

□ **automobile** 图 自動車

□ **autonomy** 图 自治(権)

□ **autumn equinox** 秋分

□ **available** 形 利用[使用・入手]できる, 得られる

□ **avatar** 图 具現, 化身

□ **avoid** 動 避ける, (～を)しないようにする

□ **Awa province** 安房地方(千葉県)

□ **awakened** 動 目覚めた

□ **awakening** 图 覚醒, 目覚め

□ **award** 動 (賞などを)与える, 授与する

□ **aware** 形 ①気がついて, 知って ②(～の)認識のある

□ **away** 熟 far away 遠く離れて

□ **awe** 图 畏敬(の念), 畏怖

B

□ **background** 图 背景, 前歴, 生い立ち

□ **backpack** 图 バックパック, リュックサック

116

- [ ] **bad luck** 災難, 不運, 悪運
- [ ] **bakufu** 幕府
- [ ] **bale** 图 俵
- [ ] **bamboo** 图 竹(類), 竹材 厖 竹の
- [ ] **ban** 图 禁止, 禁制
- [ ] **banish** 匭 追放する, 追い払う
- [ ] **bar** 图 酒場
- [ ] **barely** 圖 かろうじて, やっと
- [ ] **base** 匭《- on ~》~に基礎を置く, 基づく
- [ ] **baseball** 图 野球
- [ ] **based on** 熟《be - 》~に基づく
- [ ] **basic** 厖 基礎の, 基本の
- [ ] **basically** 圖 基本的には, 大筋では
- [ ] **basis** 图 ①土台, 基礎 ②基準, 原理
- [ ] **Bato Kannon** 馬頭観音《菩薩の一尊。観音菩薩の変化身の1つ》
- [ ] **B.C.** 紀元前, 紀元前~年(=Before Christ)
- [ ] **bead** 数珠玉,《-s》ビーズ[のネックレス]
- [ ] **bear** 匭 ~を身に着ける 图 熊
- [ ] **beauty** 图 美, 美しい人[物]
- [ ] **beforehand** 圖 あらかじめ, 前もって
- [ ] **beg** 匭 懇願する, お願いする
- [ ] **beginning** 图 初め, 始まり
- [ ] **behavior** 图 振る舞い, 態度, 行動
- [ ] **behind** 前 ~の後ろに, ~の背後に
- [ ] **being** 图 存在, 生命, 人間 **human being** 人, 人間
- [ ] **belief** 图 信じること, 信念, 信用
- [ ] **believer** 图 信じる人, 信奉者, 信者
- [ ] **bell** 图 ベル, 鈴, 鐘
- [ ] **belong** 匭《- to ~》~に属する, ~のものである
- [ ] **below** 前 ~より下に
- [ ] **beneficence** 图 供物
- [ ] **benefit** 图 利益, 恩恵 匭 利益を得る, (~の)ためになる
- [ ] **benevolent** 厖 慈善の, 慈愛の
- [ ] **benign** 厖 親切な, 温和な
- [ ] **Benten** 弁天《仏教の守護神である天部の一つ》
- [ ] **Benzaiten** 弁財天《仏教の守護神である天部の一つ》
- [ ] **bestow** 匭 (名誉などを)授ける
- [ ] **beyond** 前 ~を越えて, ~の向こうに
- [ ] **bib** 图 よだれ掛け, 前掛け
- [ ] **bill** 图 紙幣
- [ ] **bird's-eye view** 概観, 鳥瞰図
- [ ] **birth** 图 ①出産, 誕生 ②生まれ, 起源, (よい)家柄 **give birth** 出産する **give birth to** ~を生む
- [ ] **Birushana** 图 毘盧遮那仏《大乗仏教における仏の1つ。華厳経において中心的な存在として扱われる尊格。密教においては大日如来と同一視される》
- [ ] **Bishamonten** 图 毘沙門天《仏教における天部の仏神で, 四天王の一尊に数えられる武神》
- [ ] **bit** 图 ①小片, 少量 ②《a - 》少し, ちょっと
- [ ] **blank** 厖 白紙の, からの
- [ ] **bless** 匭 神の加護を祈る, ~を祝福する
- [ ] **blessing** 图 ①(神の)恵み, 加護 ②祝福の祈り ③(食前・食後の)祈り
- [ ] **bo tree** 菩提樹《クワ科の高木。ブッダがこの木の下で悟りを開いたとされ, 仏教徒にとって聖なる木となっている》
- [ ] **Bodhidharma** 图 菩提達磨(ぼだいだるま)《中国禅宗の開祖とされているインド人仏教僧》
- [ ] **Bodhisattva** 图 菩薩(ぼさつ)《いずれ如来になるべく悟りを求めながら, 人々に現世利益の福徳を授けてくれる仏》
- [ ] **bodily** 厖 身体上の, 体の

117

□ **bon-dana** 名 盆棚《お盆に先祖に供物を供えるための棚》

□ **bond** 名 結びつき, 結束

□ **bonfire** 名 (祝祭日などの) 大かがり火, たき火

□ **bonno** 名 煩悩《仏教の教義の一つで, 身心を乱し悩ませ智慧を妨げる心の働き (汚れ) を言う》

□ **Bonten** 名 梵天《帝釈天と共に仏法を守護する神。宇宙の最高原理を神格化したもの》

□ **border** 名 境界, へり, 国境

□ **bosatsu** 名 菩薩《いずれ如来になるべく悟りを求めながら, 人々に現世利益の福徳を授けてくれる仏》

□ **bottom** 名 底, 下部, すそ野, ふもと, 最下位, 根底

□ **boulder** 名 大きな丸石

□ **bout** 名 〔相撲の〕取り組み

□ **bow** 名 お辞儀, えしゃく

□ **bracelet** 名 ブレスレット

□ **branch** 名 枝 動

□ **Brazil** 名 ブラジル《国》

□ **break out** 発生する, 急に起こる, (戦争が) 勃発する

□ **bream** 名 ブリーム《コイ科の淡水魚の総称》 **sea bream** タイ (科の魚)

□ **brewery** 名 〔ビールなどの〕醸造所 **sake brewery** 酒造会社, 造り酒屋

□ **broad** 形 幅の広い

□ **brotherhood** 名 兄弟愛

□ **brow** 名 ひたい, まゆ (毛)

□ **brushy** 形 ブラシのような

□ **bucket** 名 バケツ

□ **Buddha** 名 仏陀, 釈迦《仏教の開祖》

□ **buddha-nature** 名 仏性《衆生が持つ仏としての本質, 仏になるための原因のこと。主に『涅槃経』で説かれる大乗仏教独特の教理》

□ **Buddhahood** 名 悟りの境地

□ **Buddhism** 名 仏教, 仏道, 仏法

□ **Buddhist** 形 仏教 (徒) の, 仏陀の 名 仏教徒

□ **Buddhist calendar** 仏暦 (ぶつれき)《釈迦が入滅したとされる年, またはその翌年を元年とする紀年法》

□ **Buddhist priesthood** 仏門

□ **building** 名 建物, 建造物, ビルディング

□ **burner** 名 バーナー, 火口, ガス台

□ **burning** 名 燃焼

□ **bury** 動 埋葬する, 埋める

□ **bussho** 名 仏性《衆生が持つ仏としての本質, 仏になるための原因のこと。主に『涅槃経』で説かれる大乗仏教独特の教理》

□ **but** 熟 not ~ but … ~ではなくて…

□ **butsudan** 名 仏壇

□ **byakko** 名 白虎《中国の伝説上の神獣である四神の1つで, 西方を守護する》

□ **Byakko Shinkokai** 白光真宏会

□ **Byakue Kannon** 白衣観音《日本や中国では, 三十三観音の一人に数えられる観音菩薩》

□ **byakugo** 名 白毫《仏 (如来) の眉間のやや上に生えているとされる白く長い毛》

□ **Byodoin** 名 平等院

C

□ **cabinet** 名 飾り棚

□ **calamity** 名 悲惨な出来事, 大惨事

□ **caldera** 名 カルデラ《火山の活動によってできた大きな凹地のこと》 **caldera lake** カルデラ湖

□ **calendar** 名 カレンダー, 暦 **Buddhist calendar** 仏暦 (ぶつれき)《釈迦が入滅したとされる年, またはその翌年を元年とする紀年法》

□ **call for** 〜を求める, 訴える, 〜を呼び求める

□ **call forth** 〜を生じさせる, 〜を引き出す

□ **call on** 呼びかける, 招集する, 求める, 訪問する

□ **calligraphy** 名 カリグラフィー作品, 書

□ **calm** 動 静まる, 静める

□ **candle** 名 ろうそく

□ **capable** 形 ①《be‐of 〜[〜ing]》〜の能力[資質]がある ②有能な

□ **capital** 名 首都

□ **capture** 動 捕える

□ **carry into** 〜の中に運び入れる

□ **carry out** 外へ運び出す, [計画を]実行する

□ **cassock** 名 司祭平服, カソック, 千早

□ **casual** 形 ①偶然の ②略式の, カジュアルな ③おざなりの

□ **category** 名 カテゴリー, 種類, 部類

□ **Catholic** 形 カトリックの 名 カトリック教徒

□ **cave** 名 洞穴, 洞窟

□ **celebrate** 動 ①祝う, 祝福する ②祝典を開く

□ **celebration** 名 ①祝賀 ②祝典, 儀式

□ **central** 形 中央の, 主要な

□ **centralize** 動 中心に集める, 集中させる, 中央集権化する

□ **cereal** 名 穀物

□ **ceremonial** 形 儀式的な, 公式の

□ **ceremony** 名 儀式, 式典

□ **certain** 形 ある

□ **challenge** 動 挑む, 試す

□ **challenging** 形 能力が試される, やる気をそそる

□ **champion** 名 優勝者, チャンピオ

ン grand champion 横綱

□ **Chan (Soto Zen) school** 曹洞宗

□ **Chang-weng Ju-ching** 長翁如浄（ちょうおうにょじょう）禅師《中国の南宋の曹洞宗の僧》

□ **chant** 名 詠唱 動 詠唱する

□ **chanting** 名 (経を)唱えること

□ **chaos** 名 無秩序, 混乱状態

□ **chapel** 名 礼拝堂

□ **chapter** 名 (書物の)章

□ **character** 名 ①特性, 個性 ②文字, 記号

□ **characteristic** 名 特徴, 特性, 特色

□ **charge** 動 (代金を)請求する

□ **charismatic** 形 カリスマ的な, カリスマ性のある

□ **charm** 名 まじない, お守り

□ **chase** 動 ①追跡する, 追い[探し]求める ②追い立てる

□ **chest** 名 胸

□ **chiefly** 副 主として, まず第一に

□ **chihaya** 名 千早《日本において古くから神事の際に用いられた衣装で, 主に女性が着た》

□ **child-bearing** 名 出産, 分娩

□ **childbirth** 名 出産, 分娩

□ **China** 名 中国

□ **Chinese** 形 中国(人)の 名 ①中国人 ②中国語

□ **chozuya** 名 手水舎《参拝者が身を浄めるために手水を使う施設のこと》

□ **Christian** 名 キリスト教徒, クリスチャン 形 キリスト(教)の

□ **Christian-style** 形 キリスト教式の

□ **Christianity** 名 キリスト教, キリスト教信仰

□ **chronicle** 名 年代記, 記録, 物語

□ **chrysanthemum** 名 キク(菊)

A B C D E F G H I J K L M N O P Q R S T U V W X Y Z

□ **circle** 图 円, 円周, 輪 動 回る

□ **circumference** 图 外周, 円周

□ **citizen** 图 ①市民, 国民 ②住民, 民間人

□ **civil** 形 ①一般人の, 民間(人)の ②国内の, 国家の **civil servant** 公務員

□ **claim** 動 ①主張する ②要求する, 請求する 图 ①主張, 断言 ②要求, 請求

□ **clan** 图 ①氏族 ②一家, 一門

□ **clap** 動 (手を)たたく

□ **clapping** 图 拍手, 柏手

□ **Class-A war criminal** A級戦犯《第二次世界大戦の連合国によるポツダム宣言六條に基づき, 極東国際軍事裁判(東京裁判)により有罪判決を受けた者》

□ **classify** 動 分類する, 区別する

□ **Clean Government Party** 公明党

□ **clear** 形 はっきりした, 明白な

□ **clerical** 形 書記の, 事務(員)の

□ **client** 图 依頼人, 顧客, クライアント

□ **clockwise** 形 時計回りの, 右回りの

□ **close to** 《be –》～に近い

□ **closely** 副 ①密接に ②念入りに, 詳しく ③ぴったりと

□ **clothing** 图 衣類, 衣料品

□ **collection** 图 収集, 収蔵物

□ **combination** 图 ①結合(状態, 行為), 団結 ②連合, 同盟

□ **combine** 動 ①結合する[させる] ②連合する, 協力する

□ **come down** 下りて来る, 田舎へ来る

□ **come true** 実現する

□ **comical** 形 こっけいな, コミカルな

□ **coming** 图 到来, 来ること

□ **commentary** 图 解説, 注釈書

□ **commerce** 图 商業, 貿易

□ **commit** 動 (罪などを)犯す

□ **commitment** 图 委託, 約束, 確約, 責任

□ **commonly** 副 一般に, 通例

□ **communicate** 動 ①知らせる, 連絡する ②理解し合う

□ **communication** 图 伝えること, 伝導, 連絡

□ **communion** 图 ①共有 ②親交, 交流, 交際

□ **community** 图 団体, 共同社会, 地域社会

□ **compassion** 图 思いやり, 深い同情

□ **compassionate** 形 思いやりのある, 慈悲深い, 心の優しい

□ **compile** 動 編集する, まとめる, コンパイルする

□ **complete** 形 完全な, まったくの, 完成した 動 完成させる

□ **completely** 副 完全に, すっかり

□ **complex** 形 入り組んだ, 複雑な, 複合の

□ **compose** 動 作曲する, (詩などを)書く

□ **compound** 图 囲いのある場所

□ **concept** 图 概念, 観念, テーマ

□ **concern** 動 ①関係する, 《be -ed in [with] ～》～に関係している

□ **condition** 图 ①(健康)状態, 境遇 ②《-s》状況, 様子

□ **conduct** 動 導く, 指導する

□ **conflict** 图 争い, 対立

□ **confront** 動 直面する, 立ち向かう

□ **Confucian** 形 儒教の, 孔子の

□ **Congo** 图 コンゴ民主共和国

□ **congratulation** 图 祝賀, 祝い

□ **connect** 動 つながる, つなぐ, 関係づける

- [ ] **connection** 名つながり, 関係
- [ ] **conscious** 形（状況などを）意識している, 自覚している
- [ ] **consequently** 副したがって, 結果として
- [ ] **consider** 動①考慮する, 〜しようと思う ②（〜と）みなす
- [ ] **considerable** 形相当な, かなりの
- [ ] **considerate** 形思いやりのある
- [ ] **consist** 動〔〜から〕成る, 成り立つ
- [ ] **constitution** 名憲法
- [ ] **construct** 動建設する, 組み立てる
- [ ] **construction** 名構造, 建設, 工事, 建物
- [ ] **contain** 動含む, 入っている
- [ ] **container** 名容器, 入れ物
- [ ] **contemporary** 形同時代の, 現代の
- [ ] **content** 名目次
- [ ] **contentment** 名満足（すること）
- [ ] **continuous** 形連続的な, 継続する, 絶え間ない
- [ ] **contrast** 名対照, 対比
- [ ] **contribute** 動貢献する
- [ ] **control** 動①管理［支配］する ②抑制する, コントロールする
- [ ] **controversy** 名論争, 議論
- [ ] **convert** 動改宗する
- [ ] **convince** 動納得させる, 確信させる
- [ ] **cooperation** 名協力, 協業, 協調
- [ ] **core** 名核心, 中心, 芯
- [ ] **corpse** 名（人間の）死体, 死骸
- [ ] **cosmic** 形宇宙の, 無限の
- [ ] **cosmology** 名宇宙論
- [ ] **costume** 名衣装, 服装
- [ ] **cotton** 名①綿, 綿花 ②綿織物, 綿糸

- [ ] **counsel** 動忠告する, 勧める
- [ ] **counseling** 名カウンセリング, 相談
- [ ] **count** 動①数える ②（〜を…と）みなす
- [ ] **count as** 〜と見なされる
- [ ] **counter-clockwise** 形反時計回りに, 左回りに
- [ ] **counterpart** 名対応する人［もの］
- [ ] **countryside** 名地方, 田舎
- [ ] **couple** 名①2つ, 対 ②夫婦, 一組
- [ ] **courageous** 形勇気のある
- [ ] **course** 熟 of course もちろん, 当然
- [ ] **court** 名宮廷, 宮殿 imperial court 朝廷
- [ ] **cover** 動覆う, 包む be covered with 〜で覆われている
- [ ] **covetousness** 名強欲
- [ ] **cow** 名雌牛, 乳牛
- [ ] **crane** 名ツル（鶴）
- [ ] **create** 動創造する, 生み出す, 引き起こす
- [ ] **creation** 名創造［物］
- [ ] **creator** 名創作者, 創造者, 神
- [ ] **creature** 名（神の）創造物, 生物, 動物
- [ ] **credited with** 《be –》〜の功績があると信じられている［思われている・考えられている］
- [ ] **cremate** 動火葬する
- [ ] **cremation** 名火葬
- [ ] **criminal** 名犯罪者, 犯人
- [ ] **critical** 形①批評の, 批判的な ②危機的な, 重大な
- [ ] **criticize** 動①非難する, あら探しをする ②酷評する
- [ ] **crop** 名作物, 収穫
- [ ] **crossbeam** 名横木

A
B
C
D
E
F
G
H
I
J
K
L
M
N
O
P
Q
R
S
T
U
V
W
X
Y
Z

□ **crush** 動 押しつぶす, 砕く, 粉々にする

□ **crystal** 名 水晶

□ **cucumber** 名 キュウリ

□ **cult** 名 カルト, 狂信的教団 (の信者)

□ **cultivation** 名 耕作, 栽培

□ **cultural** 形 文化の, 文化的な
Agency of Cultural Affairs 文化庁

□ **curd** 名 〔牛乳の〕凝乳, 〔凝乳状の〕凝固物 **fried soybean curd** 油揚げ

□ **curl** 名 巻き毛, 渦巻状のもの

□ **curly** 形 巻き毛の

□ **current** 形 現在の, 目下の, 通用〔流通〕している

□ **currently** 副 今のところ, 現在

□ **curse** 名 のろい (の言葉)

□ **curve** 名 曲線, カーブ

□ **curved** 形 湾曲した, 曲がった, 弓なりになった

□ **customer** 名 顧客

□ **cut off** 切断する, 切り離す

□ **cycle** 名 周期, 循環

D

□ **dai** 名 大

□ **Daibosatsu** 名 大菩薩

□ **daibutsu** 名 大仏

□ **Daigongen** 名 大権現《仏が衆生を救うために, 神・人など仮の姿をもってこの世に現れること。また, その現れたもの。権化。徳川家康の尊称》

□ **daikichi** 名 大吉

□ **Daikokuten** 名 大黒天《ヒンドゥー教のシヴァ神の異名であり, これが仏教に取り入れられたもの。七福神の一柱》

□ **daikyo** 名 大凶

□ **daily** 形 毎日の, 日常の 副 毎日, 日ごとに

□ **daimoku** 名 題目《日蓮宗で唱える「南無妙法蓮華経」の七字のこと》

□ **daimyo** 名 大名

□ **Dainichi (Nyorai)** 大日如来《真言密教の教主である仏であり, 密教の本尊》

□ **dam** 名 ダム

□ **damage** 動 損害を与える, 損なう

□ **danka** 名 檀家

□ **Daoist** 形 道教の

□ **darkness** 名 暗さ, 暗やみ

□ **daruma** 名 だるま

□ **Dazaifu** 名 大宰府

□ **Dazaifu Shrine** 太宰府天満宮

□ **death** 名 死, 死ぬこと

□ **deceased** 名《the –》故人 形 死亡した

□ **decision** 名 決定, 決心

□ **decline** 動 衰える

□ **decorate** 動 飾る

□ **decoration** 名 装飾, 飾りつけ

□ **decrease** 動 減少する

□ **dedicate** 動 捧げる, 奉納する, 献呈する

□ **deeply** 副 深く, 非常に

□ **deer** 名 シカ (鹿)

□ **defeat** 名 敗北

□ **defilement** 名 不浄, 汚染

□ **define** 動 ①定義する, 限定する ②〜の顕著な特性である

□ **definite** 形 限定された, 明確な, はっきりした

□ **definitely** 副 ①限定的に, 明確に, 確実に ②まったくそのとおり

□ **deify** 動 神格化する, 神聖視する

□ **deity** 名 神, 神性

□ **demon-god** 名 魔神

□ **deny** 動 否定する, 断る, 受けつけない

122

□ **departed** 图死者, 故人

□ **depend** 動《 – on［upon］〜》①〜を頼る, 〜をあてにする ②〜による

□ **depress** 動①憂うつにする, 落ち込ませる ②押し下げる

□ **derive** 動①由来する, 派生する ②（本源から）引き出す ③由来をたどる

□ **descend** 動①下りる ②減少する ③由来する, （子孫に）伝わる ④《be -ed from》〜の子孫である, 〜に由来する

□ **descending** 形下って行く, 下向きの

□ **describe** 動（言葉で）描写する, 特色を述べる, 説明する

□ **design** 图デザイン, 設計（図）

□ **designate** 動①示す ②（〜と）称する ③指名する

□ **desire** 图欲望, 欲求, 願望

□ **desperately** 副絶望的に, 必死になって

□ **destroy** 動破壊する

□ **detail** 图細部, 《-s》詳細

□ **detract** 動そらす, 減じる, 損なう

□ **deva** 图《ヒンドゥー教・仏教》神

□ **develop** 動①発達する［させる］②開発する

□ **devoid** 形欠けている, 欠いている

□ **devote** 動①（〜を…に）捧げる ②《 – oneself to 〜》〜に専念する

□ **devoted** 形献身的な, 熱心な, 愛情深い

□ **devotion** 图献身, 没頭, 忠誠

□ **devout** 形信心深い, 敬虔な

□ **dharma** 图《ヒンドゥー教・仏教》法, 正しい行い, 徳

□ **Dharma circle** 法座《説法の行われる集会。法席》

□ **dialogue** 图対話, 話し合い

□ **diamond** 图ダイヤモンド

□ **Diamond (Kongo-kai)** 金剛界《密教で, 大日如来の, すべての煩悩を打ち破る強固な力を持つ智徳の面を表した部門》

□ **Diamond Realm Mandala** 金剛界曼荼羅《大日如来の知徳の世界を表現したもので, 全体が九つに区切られた複合型の曼荼羅》

□ **differ** 動異なる, 違う, 意見が合わない

□ **differently** 副（〜と）異なって, 違って

□ **difficulty** 图難局, 支障

□ **dining** 图食事, 夕食をとること

□ **dining hall** 食堂（じきどう）《寺院で, 僧が, 儀式のときの斎食をなしたり, 集まって食事をする建物》

□ **direct** 形まっすぐな, 直接の, 率直な, 露骨な

□ **directly** 副①じかに ②まっすぐに ③ちょうど

□ **disappear** 動見えなくなる, 姿を消す, なくなる

□ **disaster** 图災害, 災難, まったくの失敗

□ **disciple** 图弟子, 門人

□ **discipline** 图規律, しつけ

□ **discontented** 形不平［不満］のある

□ **discourage** 動①やる気をそぐ, 失望させる ②（〜するのを）阻止する, やめさせる

□ **disease** 图病気

□ **disillusioned** 形〔真実を知って〕幻滅を感じた, がっかりした

□ **dispel** 動追い払う, （疑いなどを）一掃する

□ **dissatisfied** 形不満な, 不満そうな

□ **distinctive** 形独特の, 特色［特徴］のある

□ **distinguish** 動①見分ける, 区別する ②特色づける ③相違を見分ける

A
B
C
D
E
F
G
H
I
J
K
L
M
N
O
P
Q
R
S
T
U
V
W
X
Y
Z

□ **district** 图 地方, 地域

□ **disturb** 動 かき乱す, 妨げる

□ **divination** 图 占い

□ **divine** 形 神聖な, 神の 图 神

□ **divinity** 图 神性, 神格, 神

□ **division** 图 ①分割 ②部門 ③境界

□ **doctrine** 图 ①教義, 信条, 主義 ②政策 ③原理, 学説

□ **documented** 形 文書化された

□ **Dogen** 图 道元

□ **dohyo** 图 土俵

□ **dominant** 形 支配的な, 優勢な, (遺伝において)優性な

□ **donation** 图 寄付金, 献金

□ **donor** 图 寄贈者

□ **Donto-sai** 图 どんと祭《お正月飾りなどを燃やして新年の幸運を祈る祭り》

□ **dormitory** 图 寄宿舎, 寮

□ **Doshisha University** 同志社大学

□ **Dosho** 图 道昭

□ **dozen** 图 1ダース, 12(個)

□ **dragon** 图 竜, 辰

□ **dragon wheel** 竜車《天子の車。天子の乗り物》

□ **draw** 動 引く, 引っ張る

□ **drawing** 图 ①素描, 製図 ②引くこと

□ **drawn** 動 draw (引く)の過去分詞

□ **drawstring** 图〔袋の口などを締めるための〕引きひも

□ **drew** 動 draw (引く)の過去

□ **drinking** 图 飲むこと, 飲酒

□ **drinking gourd** ひょうたん(型)の瓶

□ **dust** 图 ちり, ほこり

□ **duty** 图 職務, 任務

□ **dynamic** 形 活動的な, 動的な, ダイナミックな

E

□ **each** 熟 each time ～するたびに on each side それぞれの側に

□ **earring** 图《通例-s》イヤリング

□ **earth** 熟 on earth ①いったい ②地球上で, この世で

□ **earthly** 形 地上の, 現世の

□ **earthquake** 图 地震, 大変動

□ **easily** 副 容易に, たやすく, 苦もなく

□ **eastern** 形 東方の, 東向きの

□ **Ebisu** 图 恵比寿《七福神の一員の中で日本古来の唯一の福の神》

□ **Echizen** 图 越前《現在の福井県》

□ **eclectic** 形 ①取捨選択する ②折衷的な, 折衷主義の

□ **ecstatic** 形 恍惚とした, われを忘れた

□ **ecumenical** 形 普遍的な, 世界的な

□ **Edo period** 江戸時代

□ **effective** 形 効果的である, 有効である

□ **effort** 图 努力(の成果)

□ **eggplant** 图 ナス(茄子)

□ **Eightfold Noble Path** 八正道(はっしょうどう)《仏教において涅槃に至るための8つの実践徳目である正見, 正思惟, 正語, 正業, 正命, 正精進, 正念, 正定のこと》

□ **Eiheiji** 图 永平寺

□ **Eisai** 图 栄西

□ **either A or B** Aかそれともか B

□ **election** 图 選挙, 投票

□ **element** 图 要素, 成分, 元素

□ **elementary** 形 ①初歩の ②単純な, 簡単な

□ **Eleven-headed Kannon** 十一面観音《観音菩薩の変化身の1つであり, 六観音の1つ。頭部に11の顔を持つ菩薩》

124

- □ **eliminate** 動削除［排除・除去］する，撤廃する
- □ **elite** 名エリート，えり抜き
- □ **elitist** 形選民的な
- □ **elsewhere** 副どこかほかの所で［へ］
- □ **ema plaque** 絵馬
- □ **embrace** 動〔主義・思想などを〕受け入れる，採用する
- □ **eminent** 形（身分などが）高い，名高い，高名な
- □ **Emma** 名閻魔《人間の生前の行為，罪の軽重を審判する，地獄の大王》
- □ **emotion** 名感激，感動，感情
- □ **emperor** 名皇帝，天皇
- □ **emphasize** 動①強調する②重視する
- □ **employee** 名従業員，会社員，被雇用者
- □ **employment** 名①雇用②仕事，職
- □ **emptiness** 名①から，空虚，無意味②空腹
- □ **enclose** 動①同封する，入れる②取り囲む
- □ **encourage** 動①勇気づける②促進する，助長する
- □ **enemy** 名敵
- □ **enlightened** 形悟りに達した，悟りを開いた
- □ **enlightenment** 名啓発，啓蒙，教化
- □ **enormous** 形ばく大な，非常に大きい，巨大な
- □ **Enryakuji** 名延暦寺
- □ **enshrine** 動〔神聖なものとして〕祭る，安置する
- □ **ensure** 動確実にする，保証する
- □ **entangle** 動（面倒なことに）巻き込む，もつれさせる
- □ **entertain** 動①もてなす，接待する②楽しませる
- □ **entire** 形全体の，完全な，まったくの
- □ **entrance exam** 入学試験
- □ **entrust** 動ゆだねる，任せる，委託する
- □ **Entsuji** 円通寺
- □ **epidemic** 名(病気の)流行，伝染病，疫病
- □ **equal** 形等しい，均等な，平等な
- □ **equinox** 名昼夜平分時 **autumn equinox** 秋分 **spring equinox** 春分
- □ **eradicate** 動根絶する，絶つ
- □ **erect** 動①直立させる②建設する
- □ **escape** 動逃げる，免れる
- □ **esoteric** 形秘伝的な
- □ **Esoteric Buddhism** 密教
- □ **essence** 名本質，真髄，最重要点
- □ **essential** 形本質的な，必須の
- □ **essentially** 副本質的に，原則的に，本来
- □ **establish** 動確立する，立証する，設置［設立］する
- □ **establishment** 名①確立，設立，発足②《the E-》体制
- □ **estimate** 動見積もる
- □ **ethics** 名倫理学，倫理(観)
- □ **eve** 名前日，前夜
- □ **even though** ～であるけれども，～にもかかわらず
- □ **eventually** 副結局は
- □ **everyday** 形毎日の，日々の
- □ **everyone** 代誰でも，皆
- □ **everything** 代すべてのこと［もの］，何でも，何もかも
- □ **evidence** 名証拠，証人
- □ **evil** 形邪悪な
- □ **Evil-destroying** 形邪悪を打ち破る
- □ **evolve** 動～を発達させる［展開す

A
B
C
D
E
F
G
H
I
J
K
L
M
N
O
P
Q
R
S
T
U
V
W
X
Y
Z

る〕

☐ **exam** 名《略式》テスト, 試験

☐ **examination** 名試験

☐ **example** 熟 for example たとえば

☐ **exceptional** 形例外的な, 特別に優れた

☐ **exceptionally** 副例外的に, 特別に, 非常に

☐ **exclusive** 形排他的な, 独占的な

☐ **exclusively** 副①排他的に, 独占的に ②もっぱら

☐ **exempt** 形免除された

☐ **exercise** 名①運動, 体操 ②練習

☐ **exile** 名追放

☐ **exist** 動存在する, 生存する, ある, いる

☐ **existence** 名存在, 実在, 生存

☐ **existing** 形現存の, 現在の, 現行の

☐ **expand** 動①広げる, 拡張[拡大]する ②発展させる, 拡充する

☐ **explanation** 名①説明, 解説, 釈明 ②解釈, 意味

☐ **expose** 動さらす, 露出する

☐ **express** 動表現する, 述べる

☐ **expression** 名表現, 表示, 表情

☐ **extended** 形延長された, 伸ばされた extended family 〔近親者を含む〕拡大家族

☐ **extinction** 名絶滅, 死滅

☐ **extinguish** 動 (火などを) 消す

☐ **extinguish** 動消す

☐ **extravagantly** 副豪勢に

☐ **eyebrow** 名まゆ (眉)

F

☐ **fact** 熟 in fact つまり, 実は, 要するに

☐ **failure** 名①失敗, 落第 ②不足, 欠乏 ③停止, 減退

☐ **faith** 名①信念, 信仰 ②信頼, 信用

☐ **faithful** 形忠実な, 正確な

☐ **falsely** 副偽って, 不当に

☐ **famine** 名飢え, 飢饉, 凶作

☐ **fang** 名牙

☐ **far away** 遠く離れて

☐ **farewell** 名別れ, 別れのあいさつ

☐ **farmer** 名農民, 農場経営者

☐ **farming** 名農業, 農作業

☐ **fear** 名①恐れ ②心配, 不安 動①恐れる ②心配する

☐ **feast** 名饗宴, ごちそう

☐ **feature** 名①特徴, 特色 ②顔の一部, 《-s》顔立ち

☐ **feeling** 名①感じ, 気持ち ②触感, 知覚

☐ **fellowship** 名①仲間, 親交 ②団体, 組合

☐ **female** 形女性の, 婦人の, 雌の

☐ **feminine** 形女性の, 女性らしい

☐ **fertility** 名肥沃さ, 繁殖力, 豊かさ

☐ **fetus** 名胎児

☐ **fierce** 形どう猛な, 荒々しい, すさまじい, 猛烈な

☐ **fiery** 形①火の, 燃えさかる ②火のように赤い

☐ **fighter** 名戦士

☐ **fighting** 形闘志あふれる

☐ **figure** 名①人 [物] の姿, 形 ②図 (形)

☐ **final** 形最後の, 決定的な

☐ **financial** 形財務 (上) の, 金融 (上) の

☐ **finial** 名相輪《仏塔最上部の装飾》

☐ **fishermen** 名漁民

☐ **Five-story pagoda** 五重塔

☐ **flame** 名炎, (炎のような) 輝き

□ **flaming** 形燃え立つ

□ **flat** 形平らな

□ **floating** 形浮いて［浮遊して］いる

□ **flood** 名洪水

□ **focus** 動①焦点を合わせる ②（関心・注意を）集中させる

□ **folk** 形民間の, 民衆の

□ **folklore** 名民間伝承

□ **followed by** その後に〜が続いて

□ **follower** 名信奉者, 追随者

□ **following** 形《the –》次の, 次に続く 名《the –》下記のもの, 以下に述べるもの

□ **for example** たとえば

□ **for oneself** 独力で, 自分のために

□ **force** 動強制する, 力ずくで〜する, 余儀なく〜させる

□ **forehead** 名ひたい

□ **forerunner** 名先駆け

□ **foretell** 動予告する, 予言する

□ **form** 名①形, 形式 ②書式 take the form of 〜となって現れる 動形づくる

□ **formal** 形正式の, 公式の, 形式的な, 格式ばった

□ **forth** 副前へ, 外へ

□ **fortune** 名①富, 財産 ②幸運, 繁栄, チャンス ③運命, 運勢

□ **foster** 動育てる, 促進させる

□ **foundation** 名①建設, 創設 ②基礎, 土台

□ **founder** 名創立者, 設立者

□ **Four Heavenly Generals** 四天王《帝釈天の配下で仏教世界を護る神。東方を護る持国天, 南方を護る増長天, 西方を護る広目天, 北方を護る多聞天からなる》

□ **Four Noble Truths** 四聖諦《仏教が説く4種の基本的な真理。苦諦, 集諦, 滅諦, 道諦のこと》

□ **fox** 名キツネ（狐）

□ **fraction** 名ごく少量, 一部分, 端数

□ **Francis Xavier** フランシスコ・ザビエル

□ **freedom** 名①自由 ②束縛がないこと

□ **fried** 形油で揚げた, フライ料理の

□ **fried soybean curd** 油揚げ

□ **frightening** 形恐ろしい, どきっとさせる

□ **from that time on** あれから, あの時以来

□ **from then on** それ以来

□ **from time to time** ときどき

□ **front** 熟in front of 〜の前に, 〜の正面に

□ **fuda** 名札

□ **Fudo Myoo** 不動明王《密教特有の尊格である明王の一尊。大日如来の化身とも言われる。また, 五大明王の中心となる明王》

□ **Fuji, Mt.** 富士山

□ **Fujiwara family** 藤原氏

□ **fuku** 名福

□ **fuku-ko-i** 福来い

□ **Fukurokuju** 名福禄寿《七福神の一神で, 福・禄・寿をさずける神。道教に由来する》

□ **fulfill** 動（義務・約束を）果たす, （要求・条件を）満たす

□ **full-fledged** 形本格的な

□ **fundamental** 形基本の, 根本的な, 重要な

□ **funeral** 名葬式, 葬列 funeral rites 葬儀 funeral service 葬儀 funeral urn 骨つぼ 形葬式の

□ **funerary** 形葬式の

□ **fusion** 名融合

□ **Fushimi Inari Taisha** 伏見稲荷大社

□ **futaku** 名風鐸《仏堂や仏塔の軒の四隅などにつるす青銅製の鐘形の鈴》

G

- [ ] **gain** 動 得る
- [ ] **gassho** 名 合掌
- [ ] **gather** 動 集まる, 集める
- [ ] **Gautama Siddharta** ゴータマ・シッダールタ, 釈迦
- [ ] **gawabashira** 名 側柱《建物の外側筋の柱のこと》
- [ ] **Gaya** 名 ガヤ《インド北東部, ビハール州中部にある宗教都市。ヒンドゥー教徒の聖地で南郊に仏教の聖地ブッダガヤがある》
- [ ] **genbu** 名 玄武《中国の神, 四象の「太陰(老陰)」, 四神の一つ, 霊獣》
- [ ] **general** 形 全体の, 一般の, 普通の
- [ ] **generally** 副 ①一般に, だいたい ②たいてい
- [ ] **generation** 名 ①同世代の人々 ②一世代
- [ ] **gentle** 形 ①優しい, 温和な ②柔らかな
- [ ] **get into** 〜に入る
- [ ] **gilt** 形 金めっきした, 金をかぶせた
- [ ] **giraffe** 名 キリン, ジラフ
- [ ] **give birth** 出産する
- [ ] **give birth to** 〜を生む
- [ ] **give up** あきらめる, やめる, 引き渡す
- [ ] **glitter** 動 きらきら輝く, きらめく
- [ ] **glutinous rice** もち米
- [ ] **go underground** 地下に潜伏する, 身を隠す
- [ ] **goddess** 名 女神
- [ ] **goen** 名 ご縁
- [ ] **gohyaku rakan** 五百羅漢《釈迦入滅後の第1回の経典結集, および第4回結集のときに集まったという500人の聖者。また, その像》
- [ ] **goju-no-to** 名 五重塔
- [ ] **gold** 名 金, 金貨, 金製品, 金色 形 金の, 金製の, 金色の

- [ ] **golden** 形 ①金色の ②金製の ③貴重な
- [ ] **golf** 名 ゴルフ
- [ ] **goma** 名 護摩《密教の秘法。不動明王などを安置し, 護摩壇で護摩木をもやしながら祈祷する》
- [ ] **goodwill** 名 好意, 親切, 善意
- [ ] **goryo** 名 御霊《怨念を持った霊のこと》
- [ ] **gourd** 名 ひょうたん
- [ ] **government** 名 政治, 政府, 支配
- [ ] **Gozan Farewell Bonfire (Gozan no okuribi)** 五山送り火《毎年8月16日に京都府京都市左京区にある如意ヶ嶽(大文字山)などで行われるかがり火》
- [ ] **gradually** 副 だんだんと
- [ ] **grain** 名 穀物, 穀類
- [ ] **grand** 形 雄大な, 壮麗な **grand champion** 横綱
- [ ] **grasp** 動 つかむ, 握る, とらえる, 理解する
- [ ] **gratitude** 名 感謝(の気持ち), 報恩の念
- [ ] **grave** 名 墓
- [ ] **gravestone** 名 墓石
- [ ] **great number of** 《a−》非常に多くの
- [ ] **greatly** 副 大いに
- [ ] **greed** 名 どん欲, 欲張り
- [ ] **greet** 動 ①あいさつする ②(喜んで)迎える
- [ ] **grill** 名 (バーベキュー用)グリル
- [ ] **growth** 名 成長, 発展
- [ ] **guarantee** 動 保証する, 請け合う
- [ ] **guardian** 名 保護者, 守護神
- [ ] **guidance** 名 案内, 手引き, 指導

H

☐ **Hachiman** 名 八幡《八幡宮の祭神。古くは皇室の祖神, 源氏の氏神として信仰され, のち, 武家の守護神となった》

☐ **haibutsu kishaku** 廃仏毀釈《明治に起こった神仏分離をきっかけに起こった, 仏教を排除しようとする運動》

☐ **haiden** 名 拝殿《神社で, 拝むために本殿の前に建てた建物》

☐ **half-bird** 形 半分が鳥の

☐ **half-man** 形 半分が人間の

☐ **half-open** 形 半開きの

☐ **hall** 名 公会堂, ホール, 大広間, 玄関

☐ **hamaya** 名 破魔矢

☐ **Hana Matsuri** 花祭《4月8日の釈迦の誕生日に修する灌仏会の通称》

☐ **hanami-do** 名 花御堂《灌仏会に誕生仏を安置する, 花で飾った小さい堂》

☐ **hand out** 配る

☐ **hang** 動 かかる, かける, つるす, ぶら下がる

☐ **Hannya Shin-gyo** 般若心経

☐ **happen to be** 偶然にも

☐ **happiness** 名 幸せ, 喜び

☐ **Hara Castle** 原城

☐ **harai** 名 祓い

☐ **hard to** ～し難い

☐ **harm** 名 害, 損害, 危害

☐ **harmony** 名 調和, 一致, ハーモニー

☐ **harvest** 名 収穫 (物), 刈り入れ

☐ **hatred** 名 憎しみ, 毛嫌い

☐ **hatsu miya mairi** 初宮参り

☐ **hatsumode** 名 初詣で

☐ **headdress** 名 かんざし

☐ **headquarters** 名 本部, 司令部, 本署

☐ **healing** 名 治療

☐ **Heart Sutra** 般若心経

☐ **heaven** 名 天国

☐ **heavenly** 形 天の, 天国のような

☐ **Heavenly Jeweled Spear** 天沼矛 (あめのぬほこ)《イザナギとイザナミが地上に降り立ち, 海をかき混ぜてオノゴロ島を作るのに使った矛》

☐ **Heian Jingu** 平安神宮

☐ **Heian period** 平安時代

☐ **height** 名 高さ

☐ **Heikenji** 名 平間寺《通称, 川崎大師》

☐ **hell** 名 地獄, 地獄のようなところ[状態]

☐ **here is ～** こちらは～です。

☐ **heresy** 名《宗教》異端

☐ **hesitate** 動 ためらう, ちゅうちょする

☐ **hibakama** 名 緋袴《腰から下に着用する和服 (袴) の一種》

☐ **hidden** 形 隠れた, 秘密の

☐ **Hiei, Mt.** 比叡山

☐ **hierarchy** 名 階級制度, ヒエラルキー

☐ **higan** 名 彼岸

☐ **highly** 副 ①大いに, 非常に ②高度に, 高位に

☐ **highway** 名 幹線道路, ハイウェー, 本道

☐ **Himalayas** 名 ヒマラヤ山脈

☐ **Hinayana Buddhism** 小乗仏教

☐ **hindrance** 名 妨害, じゃま, 障害物

☐ **Hindu** 名 ヒンドゥー教

☐ **Hirado** 名 平戸《長崎県平戸市》

☐ **historical** 形 歴史の, 歴史上の, 史実に基づく

☐ **hoji** 名 法事

☐ **hoju** 名 宝珠《仏教において霊験を

表すとされる宝の珠のこと。通常, 仏塔の相輪の最上部に取り付けられる》

□ **Hoke-kyo** 图法華経

□ **holy** 形聖なる, 神聖な

□ **honden** 图本殿《神霊を宿した神体を安置する社殿のことで, 神殿ともいう》

□ **hondo** 图本堂《仏教寺院で本尊像を安置するために造られた堂。仏殿, 金堂ともいう》

□ **Honen** 图法然

□ **honji suijaku** 本地垂迹《仏教が興隆した時代に発生した神仏習合思想の一つで, 日本の八百万の神々は, 実は様々な仏が化身として日本の地に現れた権現であるとする考え》

□ **honor** 動尊敬する, 栄誉を与える

□ **hope** 熟 in the hope of ～を望んで[期待して]

□ **hopeful** 形希望に満ちた, 望みを抱いて (いる), 有望な

□ **horin** 图宝輪《九つの輪。五大如来と四大菩薩を表す》

□ **Horse-headed Kannon** 馬頭観音《菩薩の一尊。観音菩薩の変化身の1つ》

□ **Horyuji** 图法隆寺

□ **hoshi matsuri** 阿含の星まつり《正式名「火の祭典・阿含の星まつり神仏両界大柴燈護摩供」。阿含宗最大の行事》

□ **Hosso sect** 法相宗

□ **hostility** 图敵意, 対立

□ **Hotei** 图布袋《唐代末から五代時代にかけて実在したとされる伝説的な仏僧。日本では七福神の一神》

□ **House of Growth** 生長の家

□ **household** 图家族, 世帯

□ **however** 接けれども, だが

□ **hoza** 图法座《説法の行われる集会。法席》

□ **huge** 形巨大な, ばく大な

□ **Hui-kuo** 图恵果 (えか／けいか)《中国唐代の密教僧で日本の空海の師》

□ **human being** 人, 人間

□ **hunter** 图狩人, ハンター

□ **hut** 图簡易住居, あばら屋, 山小屋

I

□ **iconography** 图図像

□ **ideal** 图理想, 究極の目標

□ **identify** 動 (本人・同一と) 確認する, 見分ける

□ **ignore** 動無視する, 怠る

□ **ihai** 图位牌

□ **illness** 图病気

□ **illogical** 形非論理的な, 筋の通らない

□ **illusion** 图錯覚, 幻想

□ **image** 图①印象, 姿 ②画像, 映像

□ **imi** 图忌み

□ **immediately** 副すぐに, ～するやいなや

□ **immovable** 形不動の

□ **impact** 图影響力, 反響, 効果

□ **imperial** 形帝国の, 皇帝の, 皇后の imperial court 朝廷

□ **impermanent** 形永続しない, 非永続的な

□ **implement** 图道具

□ **import** 動輸入する

□ **importance** 图重要性, 大切さ

□ **Important Cultural Properties** 重要文化財

□ **impressive** 形印象的な, 深い感銘を与える

□ **impurity** 图不純

□ **Inari** 图稲荷《五穀を司る神として信仰された宇賀御魂命 (うかのみたまのみこと) のこと》

☐ **Inari shrine** 稲荷神社

☐ **incantation** 图まじない, じゅ文

☐ **incarnation** 图権化, 化身, 生まれ変わり

☐ **incense** 图線香

☐ **incense burner** 香炉

☐ **include** 動含む, 勘定に入れる

☐ **including** 前～を含めて, 込みで

☐ **income** 图収入, 所得, 収益

☐ **incorporate** 動①合体させる ②法人組織にする

☐ **increase** 動増加[増強]する, 増やす, 増える 图増加(量), 増大

☐ **increasingly** 副ますます, だんだん

☐ **independent** 形独立した, 自立した

☐ **India** 图インド《国名》

☐ **Indian** 图インド人 形インド(人)の

☐ **indicate** 動①指す, 示す, (道など を)教える ②それとなく言う

☐ **individual** 图個体, 個人

☐ **industriously** 副精を出して, 勤勉に

☐ **infinite** 形無限の, ばく大な

☐ **influence** 動影響をおよぼす

☐ **influential** 形影響力の大きい, 有力な

☐ **injury** 图けが

☐ **ink** 图インク

☐ **inn** 图宿屋, 居酒屋

☐ **inner** 形①内部の ②心の中の

☐ **innocence** 图①無邪気, 純真 ②無罪, 潔白

☐ **inscribe** 〔板・石などに文字を〕刻み込む, 彫る

☐ **inscription** 图刻みつけること, 銘

☐ **insistence** 图主張, 無理強い

☐ **install** 動任命する

☐ **instead** 副その代わりに **instead of** ～の代わりに, ～をしないで

☐ **institution** 图①制度, 慣習 ②協会, 公共団体

☐ **instruction** 图教えること, 指示, 助言

☐ **integral** 形不可欠の, 肝要な

☐ **intensively** 副集中的に

☐ **interact** 動①影響しあう, 相互に作用する ②心を通わせる

☐ **interdependence** 图持ちつ持たれつの関係, 相互依存

☐ **interfere** 動①じゃまをする, 干渉する ②衝突する

☐ **International Christian University** 国際基督教大学

☐ **interpretation** 图解釈

☐ **introduction** 图紹介, 導入

☐ **intuitively** 副直観的に

☐ **invasion** 图侵略, 侵害

☐ **invoke** 動懇願する, 祈る, 訴える

☐ **involve** 動①含む, 伴う ②巻き込む, かかわらせる

☐ **involved** 形巻き込まれている, 関連する

☐ **inzo** 图印相《仏教において, 手の指で様々な形を作り, 仏・菩薩・諸尊の内証を標示するもの》

☐ **Ippen** 图一遍

☐ **Ise** 图伊勢

☐ **issue** 图問題

☐ **It is ～ for someone to ...** (人)が…するのは～だ

☐ **itako** 图イタコ《日本の北東北(東北地方の北部)で口寄せを行う巫女》

☐ **item** 图品目

☐ **itself** 代それ自体, それ自身

☐ **Izanagi no Mikoto** イザナギノミコト《日本神話に登場する男神》

☐ **Izanami no Mikoto** イザナミノミコト《日本神話の女神。イザナギ

131

ノミコトの妹であり妻》
- [ ] **Izu** 图 伊豆
- [ ] **Izumo Taisha** 出雲大社

J

- [ ] **Japan** 图 日本《国名》
- [ ] **Japanese** 圏 日本(人・語)の 图 ①日本人 ②日本語
- [ ] **Japanese-style restaurant** 料亭, 日本料理屋
- [ ] **Jesuit** 图 イエズス会の修道士
- [ ] **Jesus** 图 イエス・キリスト《前4頃 -30頃》《キリスト教の始祖》
- [ ] **jewel** 图 宝石, 貴重な人[物]
- [ ] **jeweled** 圏 宝石で飾られた
- [ ] **Ji Sect** 時宗
- [ ] **jiin** 图 寺院
- [ ] **jikido** 图 食堂《寺院で, 僧が, 儀式 のときの斎食をなしたり, 集まって食 事をする建物》
- [ ] **Jindaiji** 图 深大寺
- [ ] **jingu** 图 神宮
- [ ] **jinja** 图 神社
- [ ] **jiriki** 图 自力《自分だけの力で修行 し悟りを得ようとすること》
- [ ] **Jizo** 图 地蔵
- [ ] **Jodo Sect** 浄土宗
- [ ] **Jodo Shin Sect** 浄土真宗
- [ ] **joya no kane** 除夜の鐘
- [ ] **judge** 图 裁判官
- [ ] **Juichi-men Kannon** 十一面観 音《観音菩薩の変化身の1つであり, 六 観音の1つ。頭部に11の顔を持つ菩薩》
- [ ] **Juni Shinsho** 十二神将《仏教の 信仰・造像の対象である天部の神々で, また護法善神》
- [ ] **Jurojin** 图 寿老人《七福神の一つ。 頭の長い, 短身の老人。つえ, うちわ を持ち, 鹿を連れている。長寿を授け

る神》
- [ ] **juzu** 图 数珠

K

- [ ] **kadomatsu** 图 門松
- [ ] **kagami-mochi** 图 鏡餅
- [ ] **kagura** 图 神楽
- [ ] **kaguraden** 图 神楽殿
- [ ] **kaimyo** 图 戒名
- [ ] **kakure kirishitan** 隠れキリシタ ン
- [ ] **Kamakura** 图 鎌倉
- [ ] **Kamakura Daibutsu** 鎌倉大仏
- [ ] **Kamakura period** 鎌倉時代
- [ ] **kami** 图 神
- [ ] **kamidana** 图 神棚
- [ ] **kamisama no bunshin** 神様 の分身
- [ ] **kamishide** 图 紙垂
- [ ] **Kammu, Emperor** 桓武天皇
- [ ] **kana syllabary** 〔日本語の〕仮名 文字系
- [ ] **kanai anzen** 家内安全
- [ ] **kanbutsu-e** 图 灌仏会《釈迦の誕 生を祝う仏教行事。日本では原則とし て毎年4月8日に行われ, 一般的には 花祭と呼ばれる》
- [ ] **Kanda Myojin** 神田明神
- [ ] **Kannon** 图 観音《観世音の略称。慈 悲を徳とし, 最も広く信仰される菩 薩》
- [ ] **Kanto area** 関東地方
- [ ] **kashiwade** 图 柏手
- [ ] **Kawasaki Daishi** 川崎大師
- [ ] **Kazahino-minomiyabashi of Ise Jingu** 伊勢神宮 風日祈宮橋
- [ ] **keep track of** 〜の経過を追う. 〜の記録をつける

- □ **kegare** 名けがれ
- □ **Kenninji** 名建仁寺
- □ **kichi** 名吉
- □ **kilometer** 名キロメートル《長さの単位》
- □ **Kimmei, Emperor** 欽明天皇
- □ **kimono** 名着物
- □ **kind of** ある程度, いくらか, 〜のようなもの[人]
- □ **kindergarten** 名幼稚園
- □ **Kinkakuji** 名金閣寺
- □ **kirin** 名麒麟
- □ **kirishitan** 名キリシタン
- □ **Kisshoten** 名吉祥天《仏教の守護神である天部の1つ。もとヒンドゥー教の女神であるラクシュミーが仏教に取り入れられたもの》
- □ **Kitano Shrine** 北野天満宮
- □ **Kitano Tenmangu** 北野天満宮
- □ **known as** 《be–》〜として知られている
- □ **koan** 名公案《禅宗において雲水が修行するための課題として, 老師(師匠)から与えられる問題》
- □ **Kobo Daishi** 弘法大師
- □ **kodo** 名講堂《仏教寺院の講義, 法会のための堂》
- □ **Kofukuji** 名興福寺
- □ **Kojiki** 名古事記
- □ **Kokka Shinto** 国家神道
- □ **kokoro** 名心
- □ **kokutai** 名国体
- □ **komainu** 名狛犬
- □ **Komeito** 名公明党
- □ **kondo** 名金堂《仏教寺院で本尊像を安置するために造られた堂。仏殿, 本堂ともいう》
- □ **Kongo-kai** 名金剛界《密教で, 大日如来の, すべての煩悩を打ち破る強固な力を持つ智徳の面を表した部門》
- □ **Kongo-rikishi** 名金剛力士
- □ **Kongobuji** 名金剛峯寺
- □ **Konjin** 名金神《方位神の1つ》
- □ **Konko-kyo** 名金光教
- □ **Konpon Chudo** 根本中堂
- □ **Korea** 名朝鮮《国名》
- □ **Korean** 形韓国(人・語)の, 朝鮮(人・語)の 名①韓国[朝鮮]人 ②韓国[朝鮮]語
- □ **Korean dog** 狛犬
- □ **Korean peninsula** 朝鮮半島
- □ **koto-dama** 名言霊
- □ **kotsu anzen** 交通安全
- □ **Koya, Mt.** 高野山
- □ **Kozen gokoku-ron** 興禅護国論《栄西による仏教書》
- □ **Kublai Khan** フビライ・ハン《モンゴル皇帝》
- □ **Kukai** 名空海
- □ **kumade** 名熊手
- □ **Kumano** 名熊野
- □ **kyo** 名凶
- □ **Kyoha Shinto** 教派神道
- □ **kyozo** 名経蔵《仏教寺院における建造物(伽藍)のひとつで, 経典や仏教に関する書物を収蔵するもの》

L

- □ **laid** 動lay(置く)の過去, 過去分詞
- □ **lantern** 名手提げランプ, ランタン
- □ **lasso** 名投げ縄
- □ **latter** 形後の, 末の
- □ **Laughing Buddha** 笑い仏
- □ **lay** 形①俗人の, 在家の ②素人の
- □ **laypeople** 名素人《laypersonの複数形》
- □ **lead to** 〜に至る, 〜に通じる, 〜を引き起こす

- [ ] **leadership** 图指揮, リーダーシップ
- [ ] **least** 图最小, 最少 **at least** 少なくとも
- [ ] **leave ~ for ...** …に向けて~を去る
- [ ] **lecture** 图講義, 公演 **lecture hall** 講堂 動講義する
- [ ] **led** 動lead（導く）の過去, 過去分詞
- [ ] **legitimate** 圏合法の, 合法的な
- [ ] **length** 图長さ, 縦, たけ, 距離
- [ ] **less** 圏~より小さい[少ない]
- [ ] **Lesser Vehicle** 小乗
- [ ] **level** 图水準
- [ ] **liberty** 图自由
- [ ] **lie** 動（ある状態に）ある, 存在する
- [ ] **life** 国 **way of life** 生き様, 生き方, 暮らし方
- [ ] **lift** 動取り除く, 撤廃する
- [ ] **lightning** 图雷, 稲妻
- [ ] **like** 国 **look like** ~のように見える, ~に似ている
- [ ] **likely** 圏ありそうな, （~）しそうな
- [ ] **line** 国 **in line with** ~に沿って
- [ ] **link** 動連結する, つながる
- [ ] **lit** 動light（火をつける）の過去, 過去分詞
- [ ] **literally** 圖文字どおり, そっくりそのまま
- [ ] **literature** 图文学, 文芸
- [ ] **liturgy** 图典礼
- [ ] **living** 图①生計, 生活 ②《the -》生きている人々 圏生きている, 現存の
- [ ] **load** 動（荷を）積む
- [ ] **location** 图位置, 場所
- [ ] **logic** 图論理（学）, 理屈
- [ ] **look down** 見下ろす
- [ ] **look for** ~を探す
- [ ] **look like** ~のように見える, ~に似ている
- [ ] **look up** 見上げる, 調べる
- [ ] **loose** 圏自由な, ゆるんだ, あいまいな
- [ ] **lot** 图くじ, くじ引き
- [ ] **lotus** 图ハス（蓮）《植物》
- [ ] **Lotus Sutra** 妙法蓮華経《法華経の教え》
- [ ] **loyalty** 图忠義, 忠誠
- [ ] **luck** 图 **bad luck** 災難, 不運, 悪運
- [ ] **luxury** 图豪華さ, 贅沢（品）

M

- [ ] **made from** 《be -》~から作られる
- [ ] **made of** 《be -》~でできて[作られて]いる
- [ ] **magic mallet** 打出の小槌
- [ ] **magical** 圏①魔法の力による ②魅惑的な
- [ ] **Maha Vairocana** 大日如来
- [ ] **Mahayana** 图大乗
- [ ] **Mahayana Buddhism** 大乗仏教
- [ ] **main** 圏主な, 主要な
- [ ] **maintain** 動①維持する ②養う
- [ ] **major** 圏大きいほうの, 主な
- [ ] **majority** 图①大多数, 大部分 ②過半数
- [ ] **make ~ into** ~を…に仕立てる
- [ ] **make noise** 音を立てる
- [ ] **make sure** 確かめる, 確認する
- [ ] **make use of** ~を利用する, ~を生かす
- [ ] **Malacca** 图マラッカ
- [ ] **male** 圏男の, 雄の 图男, 雄
- [ ] **mallet** 图木槌 **magic mallet** 打出

の小槌 **wooden mallet** 杵

- [ ] **mandala** 名曼荼羅《仏教的宇宙観を描いた絵》
- [ ] **mandara** 名曼荼羅《仏教的宇宙観を描いた絵》
- [ ] **manifestation** 名表明, 明示, 声明書
- [ ] **mantra** 名マントラ, 真言
- [ ] **many** 熟 **as many as** 〜もの数の
- [ ] **mappo** 名末法《仏法が衰え, 修行して悟る者のいない時代のこと》
- [ ] **marital** 形結婚の, 婚姻の
- [ ] **mark** 名印, 記号
- [ ] **marriage** 名結婚(生活・式)
- [ ] **marry** 動結婚する
- [ ] **mask** 名面, マスク 動マスクをつける
- [ ] **masked dance** 仮面の舞
- [ ] **master** 名主人, 雇い主, 師, 名匠
- [ ] **masterpiece** 名傑作, 名作, 代表作
- [ ] **match** 動調和する, 釣り合う
- [ ] **matsuri** 名祭り
- [ ] **matter** 熟 **not really matter** たいした問題ではない
- [ ] **mausolea** 名納骨壇《mausoleumの複数形》
- [ ] **means** 熟 **by means of** 〜を用いて, 〜によって
- [ ] **media** 名メディア, マスコミ, 媒体
- [ ] **medieval** 形中世の, 中世風の
- [ ] **meditate** 動深く考える, 瞑想する
- [ ] **meditation** 名瞑想, 黙想 **seated meditation** 座禅
- [ ] **meeting** 名集まり, ミーティング
- [ ] **Meiji Jingu** 明治神宮
- [ ] **Meiji period** 明治時代
- [ ] **Meiji Restoration** 明治維新
- [ ] **Meiji Shrine** 明治神宮
- [ ] **membership** 名会員, 会員資格

- [ ] **memorial** 形記念の, 追悼の
- [ ] **memorial ceremony** 法事
- [ ] **memorial service** 法事, 法要
- [ ] **memorial tablet** 位牌
- [ ] **memorialize** 動〜を記念する
- [ ] **menace** 動おどす
- [ ] **menstruation** 名月経
- [ ] **mention** 動(〜について)述べる, 言及する
- [ ] **merely** 副単に, たかが〜に過ぎない
- [ ] **merit** 名価値, 長所, メリット
- [ ] **messenger** 名使者, (伝言・小包などの)配達人, 伝達者
- [ ] **metal** 名金属, 合金
- [ ] **meter** 名メートル《長さの単位》
- [ ] **method** 名①方法, 手段 ②秩序, 体系
- [ ] **mice** 名mouse(ネズミ)の複数
- [ ] **mid** 形中央の, 中間の
- [ ] **middle** 名中間, 最中 **in the middle of** 〜の真ん中[最中ほど]に
- [ ] **middle school** 中学校
- [ ] **middle-aged** 形中高年の
- [ ] **midnight** 名夜の12時, 真夜中
- [ ] **might** 助《mayの過去》①〜かもしれない ②〜してもよい, 〜できる
- [ ] **mikkyo** 名密教
- [ ] **miko** 名巫女
- [ ] **mikoshi** 名神輿
- [ ] **mile** 名マイル《長さの単位。1,609m》
- [ ] **military** 形軍隊[軍人]の, 軍事の 名《the–》軍, 軍部
- [ ] **military clan** 軍事氏族
- [ ] **military government** 幕府
- [ ] **Minamoto** 名源氏
- [ ] **Minamoto no Yoritomo** 源頼朝

☐ **mind** 名 心, 精神

☐ **minister** 名 ①大臣, 閣僚 **Prime Minister** 首相, 内閣総理大臣 ②聖職者

☐ **minzoku geino** 民俗芸能

☐ **miraculous** 形 奇跡の, 驚くべき

☐ **Miroku** 名 弥勒《釈迦牟尼仏の次に現われる未来仏であり, 大乗仏教では菩薩の一尊》

☐ **miscarry** 動 流産する

☐ **misfortune** 名 不運, 不幸, 災難

☐ **misogi** 名 禊《罪や穢れを落とし自らを清らかにすることを目的とした, 神道における水浴行為》

☐ **misogi harai** 禊祓《穢れを除く祓い清めの行事》

☐ **mission** 名 布教団, 伝道団

☐ **missionary** 名 宣教師, 使節

☐ **Mitaka** 名 三鷹(市)

☐ **mizuko kuyo** 水子供養

☐ **mole** 名 ほくろ, あざ

☐ **momentary** 形 瞬間的な, つかの間の

☐ **monastery** 名 修道院, 僧院

☐ **monastic** 形 修道生活の, 隠とん的な, 禁欲的な

☐ **money offering** 賽銭

☐ **Mongol** 名 モンゴル

☐ **Monju** 名 文殊《智慧を司る, 菩薩の一尊》

☐ **monk** 名 修道士, 僧

☐ **monument** 名 記念碑, 記念物

☐ **morality** 名 道徳, 徳性, 品行

☐ **more** 熟 **once more** もう一度

☐ **morishio** 名 盛り塩《塩を三角錐型あるいは円錐型に盛り, 玄関先や家の中に置く風習。主に縁起担ぎ, 厄除け, 魔除けの意味を持つ》

☐ **mortar** 名 すり鉢, 乳鉢, 臼

☐ **motivation** 名 やる気, 動機

☐ **mountain worship** 山岳信仰

☐ **mourner** 名 会葬者

☐ **movement** 名 ①動き, 運動 ②《-s》行動 ③引っ越し ④変動

☐ **mudra** 名 身ぶり《サンスクリット語》

☐ **mukaebi** 名 迎え火《お盆の時の先祖の霊を迎え入れるためにたく野火》

☐ **multiple** 形 複合的な, 多様な

☐ **Muromachi period** 室町時代

☐ **Myoho** 名 妙法《仏教において深遠微妙なる法, 教えをいう。特に『法華経』を指す》

☐ **Myoho Renge-kyo** 妙法蓮華経《法華経の教え》

☐ **myoo** 名 明王《密教における尊格及び称号で, 如来の変化身ともされる》

☐ **Myozen** 名 明全

☐ **myriad** 形 無数の, おびただしい

☐ **mysterious** 形 神秘的な, 謎めいた

☐ **mythological** 形 神話の

☐ **mythology** 名 神話

N

☐ **Nachi Falls** 那智の滝

☐ **Nakasone** 名 中曽根康弘《第71~73代内閣総理大臣》

☐ **name after** ~にちなんで名付ける

☐ **Namu Amida Butsu** 南無阿弥陀仏《名号のひとつ。「阿弥陀仏に帰依をする」という意味》

☐ **Namu Myoho Renge-kyo** 南無妙法蓮華経《日蓮宗の題目。「法華経の教えに帰依をする」という意味》

☐ **Nanzan University** 南山大学

☐ **Nara period** 奈良時代

☐ **Narita-San** 名 成田山(新勝寺)

□ **narrow** 形 狭い

□ **nation** 名 国, 国家, 《the – 》国民

□ **national** 形 国家 [国民] の, 全国の

□ **national seclusion** 鎖国

□ **National Treasure** 国宝

□ **natural setting** 自然環境

□ **naturally** 副 生まれつき, 自然に, 当然

□ **necessarily** 副 《not – 》必ずしも～でない

□ **necessary** 形 必要な, 必然の

□ **necessity** 名 必要, 不可欠, 必要品

□ **necklace** 名 ネックレス, 首飾り

□ **negative** 形 ①否定的な, 消極的な ②負の, マイナスの

□ **neighborhood** 名 近所 (の人々), 付近

□ **nembutsu** 名 念仏

□ **newly** 副 再び, 最近, 新たに

□ **newspaper** 名 新聞 (紙)

□ **Nichiren** 名 日蓮

□ **Nichiren Sect** 日蓮宗 (派)

□ **Nichiren Shoshu** 日蓮正宗

□ **Nihon Shoki** 日本書紀

□ **Nikko** 名 日光

□ **Nio** 名 仁王《仏法を護持する神である金剛力士》

□ **Nirvana** 名 涅槃《一切の煩悩から解脱した, 不生不滅の高い境地》

□ **Niwano Peace Prize** 庭野平和賞

□ **nobility** 名 ①高貴さ ②《the – 》貴族

□ **noble** 形 気高い, 高貴な, りっぱな, 高貴な **Four Noble Truths** 四聖諦《仏教が説く4種の基本的な真理。苦諦, 集諦, 滅諦, 道諦のこと》

□ **noise** 名 騒音, 騒ぎ, 物音 **make noise** 音を立てる

□ **nokyocho** 名 納経帳《寺を参拝した後にお経を書写してもらう台帳》

□ **nonbeliever** 名 〔神などを〕信じない人《ここでは仏教に帰依していない者のこと》

□ **norito** 名 祝詞《神道の祭祀において神に対して唱える言葉》

□ **northeast** 名 北東, 北東部 形 北東の, 北東部の

□ **northeastern** 形 北東の

□ **not ～ but ...** …ではなく～

□ **not really matter** たいした問題ではない

□ **nowadays** 副 このごろは, 現在では

□ **number of** 《a – 》いくつかの～, 多くの～ **a great number of** 非常に多くの

□ **nun** 名 修道女, 尼僧

□ **Nyorai** 名 如来《仏教上の最高の状態にある存在, すなわち仏のこと》

O

□ **O-bon** 名 お盆《日本で夏季に行われる祖先の霊を祀る一連の行事。日本古来の祖霊信仰と仏教が融合した行事》

□ **object** 名 ①物, 事物 ②目的物, 対象

□ **objective** 名 目標, 目的

□ **observe** 動 ①観察 [観測] する, 監視 [注視] する ②気づく ③守る, 遵守する

□ **obvious** 形 明らかな, 明白な

□ **occasion** 名 ①場合, (特定の) 時 ②機会, 好機

□ **occupant** 名 占有者, 居住者

□ **occupation** 名 職業, 仕事, 就業

□ **occupy** 動 占領する, 保有する

□ **occur** 動 (事が) 起こる, 生じる, (考えなどが) 浮かぶ

A
B
C
D
E
F
G
H
I
J
K
L
M
N
O
P
Q
R
S
T
U
V
W
X
Y
Z

- [ ] **odd** 形 奇数の
- [ ] **offer** 動 提供する〔神に祈りを〕ささげる
- [ ] **offering** 名〔神への〕ささげ物, 奉納の品 **money offering** 賽銭
- [ ] **officially** 副 公式に, 職務上, 正式に
- [ ] **ofuda** 名 お神札《神社が発行する護符の一種》
- [ ] **ohaka mairi** お墓参り
- [ ] **oharai** 名 お祓い
- [ ] **okuribi** 名 送り火《お盆の行事の一つで, お盆に帰ってきた死者の魂を現世からふたたびあの世へと送り出す行事》
- [ ] **okyo** 名 お経
- [ ] **omamori** 名 お守り
- [ ] **omikuji** 名 お御籤
- [ ] **Omoto-kyo** 名 大本 (教)
- [ ] **once more** もう一度
- [ ] **one another** お互い
- [ ] **oneself** 代 自分自身 **for oneself** 独力で, 自分のために
- [ ] **onryo** 名 怨霊
- [ ] **Ontake, Mt.** 御嶽山
- [ ] **onto** 前 ～の上へ〔に〕
- [ ] **onward** 副 前方へ, 進んで
- [ ] **open** 熟 **out in the open** 表に出して, 屋外に
- [ ] **operate** 動〔会社や組織が〕営業する, 活動する
- [ ] **opportunity** 名 好機, 適当な時期〔状況〕
- [ ] **oppose** 動 反対する, 敵対する
- [ ] **opposition** 名 反対
- [ ] **oracle** 名〔神託を授かる古代の〕神官, 巫女
- [ ] **oral** 形 口の, 口頭の
- [ ] **orchestrate** 動 調整する, 画策する, 編成する
- [ ] **ordain** 動 叙任する, 任命する
- [ ] **order** 熟 **in order to** ～するために, ～しようと
- [ ] **ordinary** 形 ①普通の, 通常の ②並の, 平凡な
- [ ] **ordination** 名 命じる行為 叙階を与える (または受け取る) 行為
- [ ] **ordination name** 戒名
- [ ] **organization** 名 組織, 団体, 機関
- [ ] **origin** 名 起源, 出自
- [ ] **original** 形 ①始めの, 元の, 本来の ②独創的な 名 原型, 原文
- [ ] **originally** 副 ①元は, 元来 ②独創的に
- [ ] **originate** 動 始まる, 始める, 起こす, 生じる
- [ ] **ornament** 名 装飾 (品), 飾り, 装身具
- [ ] **ornamental** 形 装飾の, 飾りの
- [ ] **osaisen** 名 お賽銭
- [ ] **Osaki Hachiman Shrine** 大崎八幡宮
- [ ] **Osore, Mt.** 恐山
- [ ] **Osorezan** 名 恐山
- [ ] **other** 熟 **in other words** すなわち, 言い換えれば
- [ ] **Otori Shrine** 大鳥神社
- [ ] **Oura** 大浦 (長崎県)
- [ ] **out** 熟 **out of** ①～から外へ, ～から抜け出して ②～から作り出して, ～を材料として ③～の範囲外に, ～から離れて ④(ある数) の中から **way out** 出口, 逃げ道, 脱出方法, 解決法
- [ ] **outdoor** 形 戸外の
- [ ] **outfit** 名 (ある目的のための) 服装, 装備, 道具
- [ ] **outskirt** 名 郊外
- [ ] **overall** 形 総体的な, 全面的な
- [ ] **overseas** 副 海外へ
- [ ] **own** 熟 **on one's own** 自力で

P

□ **pacify** 動 なだめる，あやす，平和を回復する

□ **pagoda** 名 仏塔

□ **painting** 名 絵画

□ **pair** 名 （2つから成る）一対，一組，ペア

□ **palace** 名 宮殿，大邸宅

□ **palanquin** 名 神輿

□ **palm** 名 手のひら（状のもの）

□ **papier-mache** 名 張り子の紙

□ **paradise** 名 天国

□ **pardon** 動 〔罪を〕見逃す，許す

□ **parent** 名 《-s》両親

□ **parishioner** 名 檀家

□ **partiality** 名 えこひいき，不公平，偏愛

□ **participant** 名 参加者，出場者，関与者

□ **participate** 動 参加する，加わる

□ **participation** 名 参加，関与

□ **particular** 形 特定の

□ **particularly** 副 特に，とりわけ

□ **partly** 副 一部分は，ある程度は

□ **pass down** （次の世代に）伝える

□ **pass on** ①通り過ぎる ②（情報などを他者に）伝える

□ **passion** 名 情熱，（〜への）熱中，激怒

□ **past** 名 過去（の出来事）

□ **path** 名 進路，通路

□ **patriarch** 名 開祖，創始者

□ **patriotism** 名 愛国心

□ **patron** 名 後援者，パトロン **patron saint** 守護聖人

□ **paw** 名 （犬・猫などの）足，手

□ **pay** 動 支払う，払う，報いる，償う

□ **peacock** 名 クジャク（孔雀）

□ **peasant** 名 農民，小作人

□ **peculiar** 形 ①奇妙な，変な ②特有の，固有の

□ **peninsula** 名 半島

□ **Perfect Liberty, the Church of** PL（パーフェクトリバティー）教団

□ **perfection** 名 完全，完成

□ **perfectly** 副 完全に，申し分なく

□ **perform** 動 ①（任務などを）行う，果たす，実行する ②演じる，演奏する

□ **performing arts** 舞台芸術

□ **period** 名 期，期間，時代

□ **permission** 名 許可，免許

□ **permit** 動 ①許可する ②（物・事が）可能にする

□ **persecution** 名 迫害，虐待

□ **personal** 形 ①個人の，私的な ②本人自らの **personal adornments** 装身具

□ **personality** 名 人格，個性

□ **pestilence** 名 疫病

□ **petition** 名 請願（書），嘆願

□ **phenomena** 名 phenomenon（現象）の複数

□ **phoenix** 名 鳳凰

□ **photograph** 名 写真

□ **phrase** 名 句，慣用句，名言

□ **physical** 形 ①物質の，物理学の，自然科学の ②身体の，肉体の

□ **pick up** 拾い上げる

□ **pile** 名 積み重ね，（〜の）山 動 積み重ねる，積もる

□ **pilgrim** 名 巡礼者，旅人

□ **pilgrimage** 名 巡礼

□ **pillar** 名 柱，支柱，支え

□ **pine** 名 マツ（松），マツ材

□ **pinwheel** 名 〔おもちゃの〕風車

□ **PL Gakuen** PL学園

□ **PL Kyodan** PL（パーフェクトリバティー）教団

A B C D E F G H I J K L M N O **P** Q R S T U V W X Y Z

□ **place** 熟 take place 行われる, 起こる

□ **plain** 形 ①簡素な ②平らな

□ **plank** 名厚板 wooden plank 卒塔婆

□ **plaque** 名額, 飾り板 ema plaque 絵馬

□ **platform** 名プラットホーム, 壇

□ **plead** 動嘆願する, 訴える

□ **pledge** 動誓約する[させる], 誓う

□ **plot** 動構想を練る, たくらむ

□ **pointed** 形先のとがった, 鋭い

□ **poison** 名 ①毒, 毒薬 ②害になるもの

□ **pole** 名棒, さお, 柱

□ **political** 形政治の, 政党の

□ **politics** 名政治(学), 政策

□ **pollution** 名汚染, 公害

□ **popular among** 《be –》～の間で人気がある

□ **popularize** 動～を世[社会]に広める

□ **population** 名人口, 住民(数)

□ **portable** 形持ち運びのできる, ポータブルな

□ **portray** 動表現する, 描写する

□ **position** 名位置, 場所, 姿勢

□ **positive** 形前向きな, 肯定的な, 好意的な

□ **possess** 動 ①持つ, 所有する ②(心などを)保つ, 制御する

□ **possibility** 名可能性, 見込み, 将来性

□ **possible** 形 ①可能な ②ありうる, 起こりうる

□ **posthumous** 形死後の[に起きた] posthumous Buddhist name 戒名

□ **posthumously** 副死後に

□ **postpone** 動延期する

□ **postwar** 形戦後の

□ **potential** 形可能性がある, 潜在的な 名可能性, 潜在能力

□ **potentially** 副潜在的に, もしかして

□ **pouch** 名小袋, 小物入れ

□ **pound** どんどんたたく, 打ち砕く

□ **pour** 動 ①注ぐ, 浴びせる ②流れ出る, 流れ込む

□ **poverty** 名貧乏, 貧困, 欠乏, 不足

□ **powerful** 形力強い, 実力のある, 影響力のある

□ **praise** 動ほめる, 賞賛する

□ **pray for** ～のために祈る

□ **prayer** 名祈り, 祈願(文)

□ **preach** 名説教 動説教する, 説く

□ **precept** 名教訓, いましめ

□ **precious** 形 ①貴重な, 高価な ②かわいい, 大事な

□ **predict** 動予測[予想]する

□ **prefecture** 名県, 府

□ **prefer** 動 (～のほうを)好む, (～のほうが)よいと思う

□ **preparation** 名 ①準備, したく ②心構え

□ **prepare for** ～の準備をする

□ **presence** 名 ①存在すること ②出席, 態度

□ **present-day** 形今日の, 現代の

□ **prevail** 動普及する

□ **prevent** 動 ①妨げる, じゃまする ②予防する, 守る, 《– ～ from …》～が…できない[しない]ようにする

□ **prevention** 名防止, 予防

□ **priceless** 形とても高価な, 金では買えない

□ **priest** 名聖職者, 牧師, 僧侶

□ **priesthood** 名司祭職 Buddhist priesthood 仏門

- □ **primarily** 副 第一に, 最初に, 根本的に
- □ **prime** 形 第一の, 最も重要な
- □ **Prime Minister** 首相, 内閣総理大臣
- □ **prince** 名 王子, プリンス
- □ **principal** 形 主な, 第一の, 主要な, 重要な
- □ **prior** 形 (時間・順序が) 前の, (〜に) 優先する
- □ **private** 形 ①私的な, 個人の ②民間の, 私立の
- □ **probably** 副 たぶん, あるいは
- □ **professional** 形 専門の, プロの, 職業的な
- □ **promote** 動 促進する, 昇進 [昇級] させる
- □ **promotion** 名 促進
- □ **propagate** 動 〔思想などを〕広める
- □ **propagation** 名 宣伝, 普及, 伝播
- □ **Propagation of Zen for the Protection of the Nation** 興禅護国論 (こうぜんごこくろん)《栄西による仏教書》
- □ **proper** 形 ①適した, 適切な, 正しい ②固有の
- □ **properly** 副 適切に, きっちりと
- □ **property** 名 財産, 所有物 [地]
- □ **proselytize** 動 改宗 [宗旨変え] を勧める, 改宗させる
- □ **prosper** 動 栄える, 繁栄する, 成功する
- □ **prosperity** 名 繁栄, 繁盛, 成功
- □ **protection** 名 保護, 保護するもの [人]
- □ **protector** 名 保護者
- □ **protest** 動 ①主張 [断言] する ②抗議する, 反対する
- □ **Protestant** 名 プロテスタント 形 プロテスタントの

- □ **prove** 動 証明する
- □ **provide** 供給する, 用意する
- □ **province** 名 地方
- □ **provoke** 動 ①怒らせる ②刺激して〜させる
- □ **public** 形 公の, 公開の
- □ **pull on** 〜を引っ張る
- □ **punishment** 名 ①罰, 処罰 ②罰を受けること
- □ **purchase** 動 購入する, 獲得する
- □ **pure** 形 ①純粋な, 混じりけのない ②罪のない, 清い
- □ **purification** 名 浄化, 精製
- □ **purify** 動 浄化する, 清める
- □ **purity** 名 汚れのないこと, 清浄, 純粋, 純度
- □ **pursue** 動 ①追う, つきまとう ②追求する, 従事する
- □ **put in** 〜の中に入れる
- □ **put on** ①〜を身につける, 着る ②〜を…の上に置く
- □ **pyramid** 名 ①ピラミッド ②角錐
- □ **pyre** 名 薪 (まき) の山

Q

- □ **quarter** 名 部署
- □ **quietly** 副 静かに

R

- □ **rack** 名 ラック, 網棚, 格子棚
- □ **radio** 名 ラジオ
- □ **rahatsu** 名 螺髪《仏像の丸まった髪の毛の名称》
- □ **rahotsu** 名 螺髪《仏像の丸まった髪の毛の名称》
- □ **railway** 名 鉄道
- □ **raise** 動 〜を育てる

- [ ] **rakan** 羅漢《「阿羅漢(仏教において最高の悟りを得た聖者)」の略称》
- [ ] **rake** 動①かき集める ②熊手でかく 名熊手, レーキ
- [ ] **random** 形手当たり次第の, 無作為の
- [ ] **range** 動①並ぶ, 並べる ②およぶ
- [ ] **rank** 名階級, 位
- [ ] **rare** 形まれな, 珍しい
- [ ] **rate** 名割合, 率
- [ ] **rather** 副①むしろ, かえって ②かなり, いくぶん, やや **rather than ~** ~よりむしろ
- [ ] **realization** 名理解, 認識
- [ ] **realize** 動理解する, 実現する
- [ ] **really** 熟 **not really matter** たいした問題ではない
- [ ] **realm** 名①領域, 範囲 ②王国, 領土
- [ ] **reason for** ~の理由
- [ ] **rebel** 名反逆者, 反抗者
- [ ] **rebellion** 名反乱, 反抗, 謀反, 暴動
- [ ] **rebirth** 名生まれ変わること, 転生
- [ ] **reborn** 形再生した, 生まれ変わった
- [ ] **recently** 副近ごろ, 最近
- [ ] **recite** 動暗唱する, 復唱する, 物語る, 朗読する
- [ ] **recognize** 動認める, 認識[承認]する
- [ ] **record** 名記録 動記録[登録]する
- [ ] **recover** 動①取り戻す, ばん回する ②回復する
- [ ] **refer** 動①《 – to ~》~に言及する, ~と呼ぶ ②~を参照する, ~に問い合わせる
- [ ] **reflect** 動映る, 反響する, 反射する
- [ ] **reform** 名改善, 改良
- [ ] **regain** 動取り戻す, (~に)戻る
- [ ] **regarded as** 《be – 》~と見なされる

- [ ] **region** 名地方, 地域
- [ ] **register** 動登録する
- [ ] **registered** 形登録された
- [ ] **registrar** 名戸籍係
- [ ] **registration** 名登録, 記載, 登記
- [ ] **regular** 形①規則的な, 秩序のある ②定期的な, 一定の, 習慣的
- [ ] **regulation** 名規則, 規定, 規制
- [ ] **reincarnate** 動~を生まれ変わらせる
- [ ] **reinterpret** 動~を再解釈する
- [ ] **Reiyukai** 名霊友会
- [ ] **reject** 動拒絶する
- [ ] **relate** 動関連がある, かかわる, うまく折り合う
- [ ] **related** 形関係のある, 関連した
- [ ] **relation** 名(利害)関係, 間柄
- [ ] **relationship** 名関係, 関連
- [ ] **relic** 名〔聖人の〕聖遺物[遺骸] **relics of the Buddha** 仏舎利
- [ ] **religion** 名宗教, ~教, 信条
- [ ] **religiosity** 名宗教性, 信心深さ
- [ ] **religious** 形①宗教の ②信心深い
- [ ] **rely** 動(人が…に)頼る, 当てにする
- [ ] **remain** 動①残っている, 残る ②(~の)ままである[いる]
- [ ] **remaining** 形残った, 残りの
- [ ] **remarkable** 形注目に値する, すばらしい
- [ ] **remove** 動取り去る, 除去する
- [ ] **repeatedly** 副繰り返して, たびたび
- [ ] **repose** 名休息, 安らぎ
- [ ] **repository** 名収納[保存]場所, 倉庫
- [ ] **represent** 動①表現する ②意味する ③代表する
- [ ] **representation** 名表現, 代表, 代理

□ **request** 图願い, 要求 (物), 需要　動求める, 申し込む

□ **require** 動①必要とする, 要する　②命じる, 請求する　**be required to** ～するように求められて [義務付けられて] いる

□ **resemble** 動似ている

□ **resent** 動不快に思う, 憤慨する

□ **reside** 動住む, 永住する

□ **resident** 图居住者, 在住者

□ **resistance** 图抵抗, 反抗, 敵対

□ **resolution** 图解決

□ **respect** 图尊敬, 尊重

□ **restoration** 图《R-》王政復古　**Meiji Restoration** 明治維新

□ **restore** 動元に戻す, 復活させる

□ **restructure** 動再編成する, 再構築する

□ **result** 图結果　**as a result** その結果 (として)　**as a result of** ～の結果 (として)

□ **resume** 動再び始める, 再開する

□ **return** 熟**in return** お返しとして

□ **reveal** 動明らかにする, 暴露する, もらす

□ **revere** 動〔神・祖先などを〕あがめる

□ **reverence** 图尊敬, 崇拝

□ **reverse** 形反対の, 裏側の

□ **review** 動①批評する　②再調査する

□ **revival** 图復活, 再生, リバイバル

□ **revolutionary** 形革命の, 画期的な, 革命的な

□ **Rice-growing season** 稲作の季節

□ **righteous** 形高潔な, もっともな

□ **righteousness** 图廉直, 高潔, 公正, 正義

□ **rigorous** 形①厳格な　②正確な, 綿密な

□ **rikishi** 图力士

□ **Rikkyo University** 立教大学

□ **ring** 图①輪, 円形, 指輪　②競技場, リング　動鳴る, 鳴らす

□ **rinse** 動ゆすぐ, すすぐ

□ **Rinzai sect** 臨済宗

□ **risky** 形危険な, 冒険的な, リスクの伴う

□ **Rissho Ankokuron** 立正安国論《日蓮が執筆し, 時の最高権力者北条時頼 (鎌倉幕府第5代執権) に提出した文書》

□ **Rissho Koseikai** 立正佼成会

□ **rite** 图 (宗教的な) 儀式　**funeral rites** 葬儀

□ **ritual** 图①儀式　②行事　③慣例

□ **riyaku** 图利益《仏の力によって授かる恵み》

□ **rokudo** 图六道《生存中の行為の善悪の結果として, 衆生がおもむく6種類の世界の状態。すなわち, 地獄, 餓鬼, 畜生, 阿修羅, 人間, 天》

□ **role** 图役割, 任務

□ **roll** 動転がる, 転がす

□ **rolled-up** 形クルクルと巻いた

□ **romance** 图恋愛 (関係・感情)

□ **roof** 图屋根 (のようなもの)

□ **rope** 图綱, なわ, ロープ

□ **rosary** 图《カトリック》ロザリオ《祈りの回数を数えるための数珠》

□ **rounded** 形〔形が〕曲線的な, 丸みを帯びた

□ **route** 图道, 道筋, 進路, 回路

□ **rub** 動こする

□ **ruler** 图支配者

□ **run out of** ～が不足する, ～を使い果たす

□ **rung** 動 ring (鳴る) の過去分詞

□ **ryusha** 图竜車《高貴な人をのせる乗り物を表す》

A
B
C
D
E
F
G
H
I
J
K
L
M
N
O
P
Q
R
S
T
U
V
W
X
Y
Z

S

- ☐ **sacred** 形 神聖な, 厳粛な
- ☐ **sadden** 動 ～を悲しませる
- ☐ **Sado** 名 佐渡
- ☐ **safety** 名 安全, 無事, 確実
- ☐ **sage** 名 賢者, 聖人
- ☐ **Saicho** 名 最澄
- ☐ **saint** 名 聖人, 聖徒 **patron saint** 守護聖人
- ☐ **saisen bako** 賽銭箱
- ☐ **sakaki** 名 榊《モッコク科サカキ属の常緑小高木。神棚や祭壇に供えるなど, 神道の神事にも用いられる》
- ☐ **sake** 名 日本酒
- ☐ **sake brewery** 酒造会社, 造り酒屋
- ☐ **sakoku** 名 鎖国
- ☐ **Sakya clan** 釈迦族
- ☐ **salary** 名 給料
- ☐ **sale** 名 販売, 取引, 大売り出し
- ☐ **saltwater** 名 塩水
- ☐ **salvation** 名 救出, 救済, 救い
- ☐ **samurai** 名 侍
- ☐ **sanctuary** 名 聖域, 禁猟区
- ☐ **sando** 名 参道
- ☐ **Sanskrit** 名 サンスクリット語
- ☐ **Sanzu no kawa** 三途の川
- ☐ **satchel** 名 学生かばん
- ☐ **satisfaction** 名 満足
- ☐ **scatter** 動 ばらまく
- ☐ **scented** 形 香りのする
- ☐ **scholar** 名 学者
- ☐ **scholarship** 名 学問, 学識
- ☐ **scripture** 名 聖なる書物, 経典
- ☐ **scroll** 名 巻物, 古文書
- ☐ **sculpt** 動 ～を彫刻する, ～の彫刻（像）を作る
- ☐ **sculpture** 名 ①彫刻 ②彫刻作品

- ☐ **sea bream** タイ（科の魚）
- ☐ **seal** 名 印
- ☐ **search** 名 捜査, 探索, 調査 **in search of** ～を探し求めて
- ☐ **seasonal** 形 季節の
- ☐ **seated meditation** 座禅
- ☐ **seclusion** 名 隔絶［隔離・隠とん］すること **national seclusion** 鎖国
- ☐ **Second World War** 第二次世界大戦
- ☐ **secret** 名 秘密, 神秘
- ☐ **sect** 名 派閥, 学派, 宗派
- ☐ **security** 名 安全（性）, 安心
- ☐ **see ～ as …** ～を…と考える
- ☐ **seek** 動 捜し求める, 求める
- ☐ **seem** 動 （～に）見える, （～のように）思われる **seem to be** ～であるように思われる
- ☐ **seen as** 《be –》～として見られる
- ☐ **Seicho no Ie** 生長の家
- ☐ **Seiganto-ji** 青岸渡寺
- ☐ **Seikyo Shimbun** 聖教新聞
- ☐ **seiryo** 名 青竜《中国の伝説上の神獣, 四神（四象）の1つ》
- ☐ **select** 動 選択する, 選ぶ
- ☐ **selection** 名 選択（物）, 選抜, 抜粋
- ☐ **self** 名 ①自己, ～そのもの ②私利, 私欲, 利己主義 ③自我
- ☐ **self-reflection** 名 内省
- ☐ **semi-government** 名 半政府［半行政・半官］
- ☐ **sendatsu** 名 先達
- ☐ **senja fuda** 千社札
- ☐ **Senju Kannon** 千手観音《六観音・七観音の一。衆生をあまねく済度する大願を千本の手に表す観音で, 千は無量円満を表す。ふつう42の手を持つ像につくる》
- ☐ **sense** 名 ①感覚, 感じ ②常識, 分別, センス ③意味

□ **Senso-ji** 名 浅草寺

□ **sentient** 形 感覚［知覚・意識］を持つ **all sentient beings** 生きとし生けるもの, 一切衆生

□ **separate** 動 ①分ける, 分かれる, 隔てる ②別れる, 別れさせる 形 分かれた, 別れた, 別々の

□ **separation** 名 分離（点）, 離脱, 分類, 別離

□ **series** 名 一続き, 連続

□ **serious** 形 重大な, 深刻な

□ **servant** 名 ①召使, 使用人, しもべ ②公務員,（公共事業の）従業員 **civil servant** 公務員

□ **serve** 動 ①仕える, 奉仕する ②（役目を）果たす, 務める

□ **service** 名 ①勤務, 業務 ②奉仕, 貢献 **funeral service** 葬儀 **memorial service** 法事, 法要

□ **set amount** 設定量

□ **set off** 出発する

□ **set out on** 〜に出発する

□ **set up** 配置する, セットする, 据え付ける, 設置する

□ **setting** 名 周囲の環境 **natural setting** 自然環境

□ **settled** 形 ［問題などが］解決している, 決着がついている

□ **Shaka** 名 釈迦《釈迦牟尼, ゴータマ・シッダールタ》

□ **shake** 動 振る, 揺れる, 揺さぶる

□ **shakubuku** 折伏《相手の悪や誤りを打破することによって, 真実の教えに帰服させる教化法》

□ **Shakyamuni** 釈迦牟尼《ゴータマ・シッダールタのこと。釈迦牟尼は「釈迦族の聖者」の意》

□ **shaman** 名 シャーマン, 祈祷師

□ **shamanistic** 形 シャーマンの, シャーマニズムの［的な］

□ **shame** 名 恥, 恥辱

□ **shape** 名 形, 姿 動 形づくる

□ **shave** 動 （ひげ・顔を）そる

□ **shelf** 名 棚

□ **Shichifukujin** 名 七福神《福をもたらすとして日本で信仰されている七柱の神》

□ **shikan taza** 只管打坐《余念を交えず, ただひたすら座禅すること》

□ **Shikoku 88-temple pilgrimage** 四国八十八箇所巡礼

□ **Shikoku hachijuhakkasho** 四国八十八箇所（巡礼）

□ **Shikoku henro** 四国遍路

□ **Shimabara Rebellion** 島原の乱

□ **shimbashira** 名 心柱《建築物, 特に仏塔などの中心となる柱》

□ **shimenawa** 名 注連縄《（神前など）神聖なものと不浄との境を示して張る縄》

□ **shin-shinko shukyo** 新新興宗教

□ **shinbutsu bunri** 神仏分離《神仏習合の慣習を禁止し, 神道と仏教, 神と仏, 神社と寺院とをはっきり区別させること》

□ **shine** 動 ①光る, 輝く ②光らせる, 磨く

□ **Shingon Sect** 真言宗

□ **shinko shukyo** 新興宗教

□ **Shinran** 名 親鸞

□ **Shinshoji** 名 新勝寺

□ **Shinto** 名 神道

□ **Shintoism** 名 神道

□ **Shitenno** 四天王《帝釈天の配下で仏教世界を護る神。東方を護る持国天, 南方を護る増長天, 西方を護る広目天, 北方を護る多聞天からなる》

□ **shobai hanjo** 商売繁盛

□ **Shobogenzo** 名 正法眼蔵《道元が, 1231年から示寂する1253年まで生涯をかけて著した87巻（＝75巻＋12巻）に及ぶ大著》

- □ **shogun** 图 将軍
- □ **shogunate** 图 将軍の職 [政治]
- □ **shore** 图 岸, 海岸, 陸
- □ **shoro** 图 鐘楼《梵鐘を掛ける寺院付属の堂舎》
- □ **Shotoku Taishi** 聖徳太子
- □ **Shotoku, Prince** 聖徳太子
- □ **shoulder** 图 肩
- □ **shown** 動 show (見せる) の過去分詞
- □ **shrine** 图 神社
- □ **shugendo** 修験道《日本古来の山岳信仰が仏教に取り入れられた日本独特の宗教》
- □ **shuin** 图 朱印《主に日本の神社や寺院において, 主に参拝者向けに押印される印章, およびその印影》
- □ **shujaku** 图 朱雀《中国の伝説上の神獣 (神鳥) で, 四神・五獣の一つ》
- □ **shuro** 图 鐘楼《梵鐘を掛ける寺院付属の堂舎》
- □ **sickness** 图 病気
- □ **side** 图 側, 横, そば **on each side** それぞれの側に **side by side** 並んで
- □ **siege** 图 包囲攻撃
- □ **sightseeing** 图 観光, 見物
- □ **significant** 形 ①重要な, 有意義な ②大幅な, 著しい
- □ **significantly** 副 大いに, 著しく
- □ **similar** 形 同じような, 類似した, 相似の
- □ **simplify** 動 簡単 [単純] にする, 平易にする
- □ **simply** 副 ①簡単に ②単に, ただ ③まったく, 完全に
- □ **simultaneously** 副 同時に, 一斉に
- □ **sin** 图 (道徳・宗教上の) 罪
- □ **sincerely** 副 真心をこめて
- □ **single** 形 たった1つの

- □ **single-minded** 形 一つの目的に向かう [ことにだけ打ち込む]
- □ **Six Nara Schools of Buddhism** 南都六宗《奈良時代, 平城京を中心に栄えた日本仏教の6つの宗派の総称。奈良仏教とも言う。三論宗, 成実宗, 法相宗, 倶舎宗, 華厳宗, 律宗》
- □ **Six Realms of Existence** 六道《生存中の行為の善悪の結果として, 衆生がおもむく6種類の世界の状態。すなわち, 地獄, 餓鬼, 畜生, 阿修羅, 人間, 天》
- □ **slightly** 副 わずかに, いささか
- □ **slogan** 图 スローガン, モットー
- □ **smoke** 图 煙
- □ **snake** 图 ヘビ (蛇)
- □ **so** 熟 **or so** ～かそこらで **so that** ～するために, それで, ～できるように **so ～ that** ～ほど～なので…
- □ **so-call** 图 いわゆる
- □ **sobo** 图 僧坊《寺院に付属した, 僧侶の住む建物》
- □ **social** 形 ①社会の, 社会的な ②社交的な, 愛想のよい
- □ **society** 图 社会, 世間
- □ **Society for the Establishment of Righteousness and Personal Perfection through Fellowship** 立正佼成会
- □ **Soka Gakkai** 創価学会
- □ **Soka University** 創価大学
- □ **sokushin jobutsu** 即身成仏
- □ **some** 熟 **in some way** 何とかして, 何らかの方法で
- □ **someone** 代 ある人, 誰か
- □ **something** 代 ①ある物, 何か ②いくぶん, 多少
- □ **sometime** 副 いつか, そのうち
- □ **sometimes** 副 時々, 時たま
- □ **somewhat** 副 いくらか, やや, 多少

146

- [ ] **soothe** 動 なだめる, 慰める
- [ ] **Sophia University** 上智大学
- [ ] **sorin** 名 相輪《五重塔などの仏塔の屋根から天に向かって突き出した金属製の部分の総称》
- [ ] **sort** 名 種類, 品質 **a sort of** 〜のようなもの, 一種の〜
- [ ] **Soto sect** 曹洞宗
- [ ] **Soto Zen** 曹洞宗
- [ ] **sotoba** 名 卒塔婆《供養のために経文や題目などを書き, お墓の後ろに立てる塔の形をした縦長の木片》
- [ ] **soul** 名 ①魂 ②精神, 心
- [ ] **source** 名 源, 原因, もと
- [ ] **Southeast Asia** 東南アジア
- [ ] **soybean** 名 大豆
- [ ] **soybean curd** 豆腐 **fried soybean curd** 油揚げ
- [ ] **sparrow** 名 スズメ (雀)
- [ ] **spear** 名 槍, 投げ槍 **Heavenly Jeweled Spear** 天沼矛 (あめのぬほこ)《イザナギとイザナミが地上に降り立ち, 海をかき混ぜてオノゴロ島を作るのに使った矛》
- [ ] **specially** 副 特別に
- [ ] **specific** 形 明確な, はっきりした, 具体的な
- [ ] **spectacular** 形 壮観な
- [ ] **spiral** 形 らせん状の, 渦巻き型の
- [ ] **spirit** 名 ①霊 ②精神, 気力
- [ ] **spiritual** 形 精神の, 精神的な, 霊的な
- [ ] **Spiritual-Friends-Association** 霊友会
- [ ] **splendid** 形 見事な, 壮麗な, 堂々とした
- [ ] **sponsor** 動 スポンサーになる, 出資する
- [ ] **sprang** 動 spring (跳ねる) の過去
- [ ] **sprig** 名〔折り取られた〕小枝
- [ ] **spring equinox** 春分

- [ ] **spring up** (急に) 生じる, (ひょっこり) 現れる
- [ ] **sprinkle** 動 振りかける, 散布する
- [ ] **Sri Lanka** スリランカ
- [ ] **staff** 名〔歩行用の〕つえ, ステッキ
- [ ] **stage** 名 ①舞台 ②段階
- [ ] **standard** 形 標準の
- [ ] **stare** 動 じっと [じろじろ] 見る
- [ ] **state** 名 国家, (アメリカなどの) 州
- [ ] **statistical** 形 統計の, 統計に基づく
- [ ] **statistics** 名 統計 (学), 統計資料
- [ ] **statue** 名 像
- [ ] **steamed** 形 蒸し加熱した
- [ ] **stern** 形 厳格な, 厳しい
- [ ] **stick** 名 棒, 杖 動 突き出る **stick out of** 〜から突き出す
- [ ] **sticker** 名 ステッカー
- [ ] **stinginess** 名 けち, しみったれていること
- [ ] **stomach** 名 胃, 腹
- [ ] **stone** 名 石, 小石
- [ ] **strand** 名 より糸
- [ ] **straw** 名 麦わら, ストロー
- [ ] **streamer** 名 吹き流し
- [ ] **strengthen** 動 強くする, しっかりさせる
- [ ] **stress** 動 強調する
- [ ] **strictly** 副 厳しく, 厳密に
- [ ] **string** 名 ①ひも, 糸, 弦 ②一連, 一続き
- [ ] **strip** 名 (細長い) 1片
- [ ] **structure** 名 建造物
- [ ] **stuck** 動 stick (刺さる) の過去, 過去分詞
- [ ] **stupa** 名 仏舎利塔《仏舎利 (釈迦の遺骨) を納めるとされる仏塔》
- [ ] **style** 名 やり方, 流儀, 様式, スタイル

147

A B C D E F G H I J K L M N O P Q R **S** T U V W X Y Z

□ **Styx, River** 名 スティックス川, 三途の川

□ **substitute** 名 代用品, 代理人

□ **success** 名 成功, 幸運, 上首尾

□ **successful** 形 成功した, うまくいった

□ **successor** 名 後継者, 相続人, 後任者

□ **such as** たとえば〜, 〜のような

□ **suffer** 動 ①（苦痛・損害などを）受ける, こうむる ②（病気に）なる, 苦しむ, 悩む

□ **suffering** 名 苦痛, 苦しみ, 苦難

□ **Sugawara no Michizane** 菅原道真

□ **suggest** 動 ①提案する ②示唆する

□ **suien** 名 水煙《火炎の透し彫のデザインだが, 火を嫌うことから水煙と呼ばれる》

□ **summon** 動 呼び出す, 要求する

□ **sumo** 名 相撲

□ **supernatural** 名 超自然の

□ **superstar** 名 スーパースター, 大スター

□ **support** 動 ①支える, 支持する ②養う, 援助する 名 ①支え, 支持 ②援助, 扶養

□ **suppose** 動 ①仮定する, 推測する ②《be -d to 〜》〜することになっている, 〜するものである

□ **supposedly** 副 たぶん, 仮に, 推定では

□ **suppress** 動 抑える, 抑圧する

□ **suppression** 名 鎮圧, 抑制, 隠蔽

□ **sure** 熟 make sure 確かめる, 確認する to be sure 確かに, なるほど

□ **surface** 名 表面

□ **surprising** 形 驚くべき, 意外な

□ **surround** 動 囲む, 包囲する

□ **surrounding** 名 《-s》周囲の状況, 環境

□ **survey** 名 調査

□ **Susanoo no Mikoto** スサノオノミコト《日本神話の神。多くの乱暴を行ったため, 天照大神が天の岩屋にこもり, 高天原から追放された》

□ **suspect** 動 疑う, （〜ではないかと）思う

□ **sutra** 名 経典

□ **suzu** 名 鈴

□ **sword** 名 剣, 刀

□ **syllabary** 名 音節文字表 kana syllabary〔日本語の〕仮名文字系

□ **symbol** 名 シンボル, 象徴

□ **symbolic** 形 象徴する, 象徴的な

□ **symbolically** 副 象徴的に

□ **symbolize** 動 ①記号を用いる ②象徴する, 象徴とみなす

□ **symmetrical** 形 〔左右や上下の形が〕対称な

□ **syncretist sect of Shinto** 教派神道連合会の一派

T

□ **T'ang** 名 唐

□ **T'ien-t'ai** 名 天台（宗）

□ **ta-no-kami** 田の神《日本の農耕民の間で, 稲作の豊凶を見守り, あるいは, 稲作の豊穣をもたらすと信じられてきた神》

□ **tablet** 名 タブレット, 銘板 memorial tablet 位牌

□ **tai** 名 鯛

□ **Taira no Masakado** 平将門

□ **taisha** 名 大社

□ **Taishakuten** 名 帝釈天《仏教の守護神である天部の一つ》

□ **Taizo-kai** 名 胎蔵界《密教における二つの世界の一つ。蓮華や母胎が種子を生育するように, 人の仏性を育て,

仏とする理法の世界》

- [ ] **takarabune** 名宝船《七福神や八仙が乗る宝物を積み込んだ帆船》
- [ ] **take down** 下げる、降ろす
- [ ] **take off** 《衣服を》脱ぐ、取り去る、～を取り除く
- [ ] **take place** 行われる、起こる
- [ ] **take the form of** ～となって現れる
- [ ] **talent** 名才能、才能ある人
- [ ] **talisman** 名お守り、護符
- [ ] **tama-gushi** 名玉串《神さまが宿るとされる榊（さかき）という木の枝に、紙垂（しで）や麻を結びつけたもの》
- [ ] **Taoist** 名道教
- [ ] **tariki** 名他力《衆生を悟りに導く仏・菩薩の力、仏・菩薩の加護のこと》
- [ ] **tassel** 名房、飾り房
- [ ] **tatari** 名祟り《神仏や霊魂などの超自然的存在が人間に災いを与えること》
- [ ] **Tathagata** 名如来《仏教上の最高の状態にある存在、すなわち仏のこと》
- [ ] **tax** 名税
- [ ] **taxation** 名課税、徴税
- [ ] **teaching** 名①教えること、教授、授業 ②《-s》教え、教訓
- [ ] **tembu** 名天部《仏教において天界に住む者の総称》
- [ ] **temple** 名寺、神殿
- [ ] **tend** 動《～の》傾向がある、《～》しがちである
- [ ] **Tendai sect** 天台宗
- [ ] **tengu** 名天狗《日本の民間信仰において伝承される神や妖怪ともいわれる伝説上の生き物。鼻が長いことが特徴》
- [ ] **Tenman Tenjin** 天満天神《菅原道真の霊を神格化した呼称。また、それをまつる神社》
- [ ] **Tenri Central Library** 天理図書館

- [ ] **Tenri City** 天理市（奈良県）
- [ ] **Tenri University** 天理大学
- [ ] **Tenrikyo** 天理教
- [ ] **tera** 寺
- [ ] **term** 名語、用語
- [ ] **thankfulness** 名感謝（の気持ち）
- [ ] **thanksgiving** 名感謝
- [ ] **that** 熟 so that ～するために、それで、～できるように so ～ that … 非常に～なので…
- [ ] **then** 熟 from then on それ以来
- [ ] **Theravada** 名上座部仏教、小乗仏教
- [ ] **thereby** 副それによって、それに関して
- [ ] **therefore** 副したがって、それゆえ、その結果
- [ ] **thick** 形太い、厚い
- [ ] **think of** ～のことを考える、～を思いつく、考え出す
- [ ] **those who** ～する人々
- [ ] **though** 接①～にもかかわらず、～だが ②たとえ～でも even though ～であるけれども、～にもかかわらず
- [ ] **Thousand-armed Kannon** 千手観音《六観音・七観音の一。衆生をあまねく済度する大願を千本の手に表す観音で、千は無量円満を表す。ふつう42の手を持つ像につくる》
- [ ] **threat** 名おどし、脅迫
- [ ] **Three-story pagoda** 三重塔
- [ ] **throughout** 前①～中、～を通じて ②～のいたるところに
- [ ] **thrown** 動 throw（投げる）の過去分詞
- [ ] **thunder** 名雷、雷鳴
- [ ] **tiger** 名トラ（虎）
- [ ] **tile** 名タイル、瓦
- [ ] **time** 熟 each time ～するたびに

A
B
C
D
E
F
G
H
I
J
K
L
M
N
O
P
Q
R
S
T
U
V
W
X
Y
Z

from that time on あれから, あの
時以来 from time to time ときどき

- □ **tip** 動 傾ける, 倒す **tip over** 〜をひ
  っくり返す, 〜を転倒させる
- □ **title** 名 ①題目, タイトル ②肩書,
  称号
- □ **Todaiji** 名 東大寺
- □ **Toji** 名 東寺
- □ **Tojo Hideki** 東条英機
- □ **Tokugawa Ieyasu** 徳川家康
- □ **Tokugawa period** 江戸時代
- □ **Tokugawa shogun** 徳川将軍
- □ **Tokugawa shogunate** 徳川幕
  府
- □ **Tokyo** 名 東京《地名》
- □ **tomb** 名 墓穴, 墓石, 納骨堂
- □ **tombstone** 名 墓石
- □ **ton** 名 ①トン《重量・容積単位》②
  《-s》たくさん
- □ **Tondabayashi** 名 富田林市(大阪
  府)
- □ **toothpick** 名 つまようじ, ようじ
  入れ
- □ **top** 熟 **on top of** 〜の上(部)に
- □ **top-ranked** 形 一流の
- □ **Tori-no-ichi** 名 酉の市《例年11月
  の酉の日に行われる祭》
- □ **torii** 名 鳥居
- □ **torikumi** 名 取り組み
- □ **tortoise** 名 カメ(亀)
- □ **Toshigami-sama** 名 歳神様《正
  月に家々に迎えて祭る神。豊作の守り
  神であり, 祖霊であるともいわれる》
- □ **Toshogu shrine** 日光東照宮
- □ **totally** 副 全体的に, すっかり
- □ **tour bus** 観光バス
- □ **tourist** 名 旅行者, 観光客
- □ **tournament** 名 トーナメント
- □ **Toyotomi Hideyoshi** 豊臣秀吉
- □ **trace** 動 たどる

- □ **track** 通った跡 **keep track of**
  〜の経過を追う, 〜の記録をつける
- □ **trade** 名 取引, 貿易, 商業
- □ **tradition** 名 伝統, 伝説, しきたり
- □ **traditional** 形 伝統的な
- □ **training** 名 トレーニング, 訓練
- □ **transform** 動 ①変形[変化]する,
  変える ②変換する
- □ **translate** 動 ①翻訳する, 訳す ②
  変える, 移す
- □ **transmission** 名 送信, 伝送, 通
  信
- □ **transmit** 動 ①送る ②伝える, 伝
  わる
- □ **transport** 動 輸送[運送]する
- □ **transportation** 名 交通(機関),
  輸送手段
- □ **trash** 名 くず, ごみ
- □ **traveler** 名 旅行者
- □ **treasure** 名 財宝, 貴重品, 宝物
  National Treasure 国宝 **treasure
  ship** 宝船《七福神や八仙が乗る宝物
  を積み込んだ帆船》
- □ **treasury** 名 宝庫
- □ **Treasury of the True
  Dharma Eye** 正法眼蔵《道元が,
  1231年から示寂する1253年まで生涯
  をかけて著した87巻(=75巻+12巻)
  に及ぶ大著》
- □ **treat** 動 扱う
- □ **treatise** 論文, 論説 **Treatise on
  the Establishment of the True
  Dharma and the Peace of the
  Nation** 立正安国論
- □ **trousers** 名 ズボン
- □ **true** 熟 **come true** 実現する
- □ **trust** 動 信用[信頼]する, 委託する
- □ **truth** 名 ①真理, 事実, 本当 ②誠実,
  忠実さ **Four Noble Truths** 四聖諦
  《仏教が説く4種の基本的な真理。苦諦,
  集諦, 滅諦, 道諦のこと》
- □ **Tsurugaoka Hachimangu**

鶴岡八幡宮

□ **turn into** 〜に変わる

□ **turtle** 名ウミガメ (海亀)

□ **tutelary** 形守護者[神]の働きをする

□ **twice-a-year** 形年に2回ある

□ **twist** 名ねじれ, 思わぬ[意外な]展開[発展]

□ **twisted** 形ねじれた

□ **two-dimensional** 形2次元の

□ **typhoon** 名台風

□ **typical** 形典型的な, 象徴的な

U

□ **Uji** 名宇治

□ **ultimate** 形最終の, 究極の

□ **uncleanliness** 名不潔

□ **undergo** 動経験する, 被る, 耐える

□ **underground** 副隠れて, ひそかに, こっそりと **go underground** 地下に潜伏する, 身を隠す

□ **underlie** 動基礎となる, 下に横たわる

□ **understanding** 名理解, 意見の一致, 了解

□ **undertake** 動始める, 企てる

□ **underworld** 名黄泉の国

□ **unexpected** 形思いがけない, 予期しない

□ **unfulfilled** 形満たされていない

□ **unhappiness** 名不運, 不幸

□ **unhappy** 形不運な, 不幸な

□ **unique** 形唯一の, ユニークな, 独自の

□ **uniqueness** 名唯一, 独自性, ユニークさ

□ **United States** 名アメリカ合衆国《国名》

□ **universe** 名《the – /the U-》宇宙, 全世界

□ **university** 名 (総合)大学

□ **unknown** 形知られていない, 不明の

□ **unless** 接もし〜でなければ, 〜しなければ

□ **unlike** 形似ていない, 違った 前〜と違って

□ **unlimited** 形無限の, 果てしない

□ **unlucky** 形①不運な ②不吉な, 縁起の悪い

□ **unpleasant** 形不愉快な, 気にさわる, いやな, 不快な

□ **unsuccessful** 形失敗の, 不成功の

□ **upon** 前①《場所・接触》〜 (の上)に ②《日・時》〜に ③《関係・従事》〜に関して, 〜について, 〜して

□ **upright** 副まっすぐ立って, 直立して

□ **uprising** 名反乱, 暴動, 謀反

□ **upward** 副上の方へ, 上向きに

□ **Urakami** 浦上 (村) (長崎県)

□ **urn** 名骨つぼ **funeral urn** 骨つぼ

□ **use** 熟 **make use of** 〜を利用する, 〜を生かす

□ **used** 動①use (使う)の過去, 過去分詞 ②《– to》よく〜したものだ, 以前は〜であった 形①慣れている, 《get [become] – to》〜に慣れてくる ②使われた, 中古の

□ **usual** 形通常の, いつもの, 平常の, 普通の

V

□ **Vairocana** 名毘盧遮那仏 (びるしゃなぶつ)《大乗仏教における仏の1つ。華厳経において中心的な存在として扱われる尊格。密教においては大日如来と同一視される》

151

□ **valuable** 形 貴重な, 価値のある, 役に立つ

□ **variety** 名 ①変化, 多様性, 寄せ集め ②種類

□ **various** 形 変化に富んだ, さまざまの, たくさんの

□ **varnished** 形 ニス塗装を施した

□ **vary** 動 変わる, 変える, 変更する, 異なる

□ **vehicle** 名 乗り物, 車, 車両

□ **veneration** 名 尊敬の念

□ **vengeance** 名 復讐, あだ討ち

□ **vengeful** 形 復讐(心)に燃えた

□ **verbal** 形 言葉の, 口頭の

□ **vertical** 形 垂直の, 縦の

□ **victory** 名 勝利, 優勝

□ **viewpoint** 名 見地, 観点, 見解

□ **violence** 名 暴力, 乱暴

□ **virtually** 副 事実上, ほぼ, 〜も同然で

□ **visitor** 名 訪問客

□ **visual** 形 視覚の, 視力の, 目に見える

□ **vitality** 名 活力, バイタリティー, 元気

□ **vow** 名 誓い, 誓約

W

□ **wand** 名 杖, 指揮棒

□ **war dead** 戦没者

□ **ward** 動 防ぐ, 寄せ付けない **ward off** 清める, 払い除ける

□ **warning** 名 警告, 警報

□ **warrior** 名 戦士, 軍人

□ **watch over** 見守る, 見張る

□ **waterfall** 名 滝

□ **wave** 動 ①揺れる, 揺らす, 波立つ ②(手などを振って)合図する

□ **way** 熟 **by way of** 〜を通って, 〜経由で **in some way** 何とかして, 何らかの方法で **on one's way** 途中で **on one's way out** 出ていくときに **way of** 〜する方法 **way of life** 生き様, 生き方, 暮らし方 **way out** 出口, 逃げ道, 脱出方法, 解決法 **way to** 〜する方法

□ **wayfaring** 名 徒歩旅行 形 徒歩旅行中の

□ **wealth** 名 富, 財産

□ **weapon** 名 武器, 兵器

□ **wedding** 名 結婚式, 婚礼

□ **weed** 動 草取りをする, (不要なものを)取り除く

□ **weeklong** 形 1週間にわたる

□ **weigh** 動 重さが〜ある

□ **weight** 動 重みをつける

□ **welfare** 名 幸福, 繁栄

□ **well-being** 名 健康で安心なこと, 満足できる生活状態, 幸福

□ **well-known** 形 よく知られた, 有名な

□ **Western** 形 西洋の

□ **What (〜) for?** 何のために, なぜ

□ **wheel** 名 輪, 車輪

□ **whether** 接 〜かどうか, 〜かまたは…, 〜であろうとなかろうと

□ **which** 熟 **of which** 〜の中で

□ **white-robed** 形 白衣をまとった

□ **who** 熟 **those who** 〜する人々

□ **whole** 形 全体の, すべての, 完全な, 満〜, 丸〜 《the −》全体, 全部 **as a whole** 全体として

□ **whom** 代 ①誰を[に] ②《関係代名詞》〜するところの人, そしてその人を

□ **widely** 副 広く, 広範囲にわたって

□ **wind-bell** 名 風鈴

□ **wine** 名 ワイン, ぶどう酒

□ **wing** 名 翼, 羽

152

□ **wire** 图 針金

□ **wisdom** 图 知恵, 賢明（さ）

□ **withdrawal** 图 引っ込めること, 引っ込むこと

□ **within** 前 ①〜の中［内］に, 〜の内部に ②〜以内で, 〜を越えないで

□ **womb** 图 子宮

□ **Womb Realm Mandala** 胎蔵曼荼羅《大日経に基づいて, 大日如来を主尊とし, その分身・眷属・護法諸尊を四方に図式的に配したもの》

□ **wonder** 動 ①不思議に思う,（〜に）驚く ②（〜かしらと）思う **wonder about** 〜について知りたがる

□ **wooden** 形 木製の, 木でできた **wooden mallet** 杵 **wooden mortar** 臼 **wooden plank** 卒塔婆

□ **words** 熟 **in other words** すなわち, 言い換えれば

□ **works of art** 芸術作品

□ **World War II** 第二次世界大戦

□ **worldly** 形 現世の, 世俗的な

□ **worship** 图 崇拝, 礼拝, 参拝 **mountain worship** 山岳信仰 動 崇拝する, 礼拝［参拝］する, 拝む

□ **worshipper** 图 礼拝者

□ **worst** 形《the −》最も悪い, いちばんひどい

□ **woven** 動 weave（織る）の過去分詞

□ **wrestler** 图 レスリング選手

X

□ **Xavier, Francis** フランシスコ・ザビエル

Y

□ **yakudoshi** 图 厄年《日本などで厄災が多く降りかかるとされる年齢のこと》

□ **Yakushi** 图 薬師（如来）《薬壺を持ち病気を治す仏様として知られる, 如来の一尊》

□ **Yakushi Nyorai** 薬師如来《薬壺を持ち病気を治す仏様として知られる, 如来の一尊》

□ **yama-no-kami** 图 山の神《山に宿る神の総称である》

□ **yamabushi** 图 山伏《修験道の行者》

□ **yao-yorozu-no-kami** 图 八百万の神《神道で数多くの神々の存在を総称していうもの》

□ **Yasaka Shrine** 八坂神社

□ **Yasukuni Shrine** 靖国神社

□ **yatsu no hokori** 八つのほこり《をしい, ほしい, にくい, かわい, うらみ, はらだち, よく, こうまん》

□ **yokozuna** 图 横綱

□ **yomi no kuni** 黄泉の国

□ **yorishiro** 图 依り代《神霊が依り憑く対象物のこと》

□ **yugyo shonin** 遊行上人《時宗集団における指導者に対する敬称。一遍, その弟子である他阿を指す事が多い》

□ **Yushima Tenjin** 湯島天神

Z

□ **Zen** 图 禅

□ **Zentsuji** 善通寺市（香川県）

□ **zigzag** 形 ジグザグの

□ **zodiac** 图 黄道帯, 十二宮図

153

English Conversational Ability Test
国際英語会話能力検定

● E-CATとは…
英語が話せるようになるための
テストです。インターネット
ベースで、30分であなたの発
話力をチェックします。

www.ecatexam.com

● iTEP®とは…
世界各国の企業、政府機関、アメリカの大学
300校以上が、英語能力判定テストとして採用。
オンラインによる90分のテストで文法、リー
ディング、リスニング、ライティング、スピー
キングの5技能をスコア化。iTEP®は、留学、就
職、海外赴任などに必要な、世界に通用する英
語力を総合的に評価する画期的なテストです。

www.itepexamjapan.com

ラダーシリーズ
Japanese Religion 日本の宗教

2020 年 6 月 5 日 第 1 刷発行

著　者　ジェームス・M・バーダマン

発行者　浦　晋亮

発行所　**IBC パブリッシング株式会社**
　　　　〒162-0804 東京都新宿区中里町 29 番 3 号
　　　　菱秀神楽坂ビル 9 F
　　　　Tel. 03-3513-4511　Fax. 03-3513-4512
　　　　www.ibcpub.co.jp

印　　刷　株式会社シナノパブリッシングプレス
装　　丁　伊藤　理恵
カバー写真　水野克比古
本文イラスト　テッド高橋

落丁本・乱丁本は、小社宛にお送りください。送料小社負担にてお取り替えいたし
ます。本書の無断複写（コピー）は著作権法上での例外を除き禁じられています。

Printed in Japan
ISBN978-4-7946-0627-3